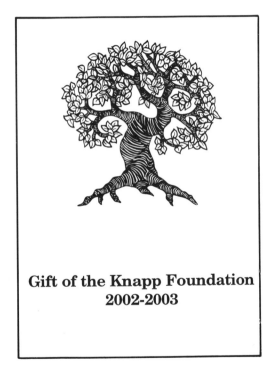

New England

Nature
WATCH

New England

Nature
WATCH

BY TOM LONG Illustrations by Jay J. Johnson

For Stacy and Sam

Library of Congress Cataloging-in-Publication Data
Long, Tom, (Thomas Francis), 1950–
   New England nature watch / Tom Long ; illustrations by Jay J. Johnson.
      p. cm.
   ISBN 1-889833-59-2
   1. Natural history — New England. 2. Seasons — New England. I. Title.
   QH104.5.N4L66 2003
      508.74—dc21   2002155464

Design by Laura McFadden Design, Inc.
Cover illustration: "Two Fawns Jumping," oil painting by Jay J. Johnson. Interior illustrations were rendered using mixed media of watercolor, pencil, and acrylic paint. To view more of Jay Johnson's artwork, visit his Web site: www.jayjjohnson.com.

Printed in Canada.

Published by Commonwealth Editions,
an imprint of Memoirs Unlimited, Inc.,
266 Cabot Street, Beverly, Massachusetts 01915.

Visit our Web site: www.commonwealtheditions.com.

CONTENTS

THANKS TO TWENTY-FOUR HOUR INTERNET ACCESS
and nonstop cable television, we've become more
familiar with the exotic side of nature than the every-
day events outdoors. Kids are more knowledgeable
about Indonesian Komodo dragons and Australian
crocodiles than about the chipmunks that chatter
behind the garage. Their parents know more about
the beasts they might encounter on an African safari
than they do about the critters that slither in local
swamps.

Nature isn't something you experience through a
television; it's right out there in your own backyard.
Those of us who are lucky enough to live in New
England have front-row seats to a full calendar of

natural dramas that play themselves out every second of every day, whether on Cape Cod, where black-backed pilot whales beach themselves in solidarity with stranded mates; or in an abandoned pasture in Greenwich, Connecticut, where mouselike shrews form a conga line that resembles a snake and thus ward off predators; or under a median strip in Newport, Rhode Island, where an ant imprisons an aphid and "milks" it of honeydew to feed the ant colony nearby. 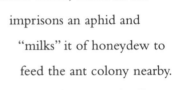 This book is a distillation of observations made over a lifetime of hiking and camping in New England—and just looking out the window of my home in New Hampshire. They're observations any amateur might make with a good pair of binoculars and a shelf full of guide books. Many of the items first appeared in the "Nature Watch" column I've written for the *Boston Globe* for several years.

It's not intended as a trail guide. It's a book you might curl up with when nature beckons, but time does not permit a foray into the field. Or you might read it to the kids—or encourage them to read it for themselves—to give them a taste of the outdoors.

From the fragrant clam flats of Narragansett Bay to the wind-wracked summit of Mount Washington, the amazing variety of plants and animals that make New England their home have lives every bit as fascinating as anything you'll see on the Discovery Channel. We're going to take a tour, day by day. We begin in the month of May, when our ancestors danced around maypoles in celebration of spring.

New England

Nature
WATCH

MAY IS FOR THE BIRDS. EACH MORNING, THE DAWN chorus grows louder as more winter migrants muscle their way up the Atlantic Flyway to join the chickadees, cardinals, nuthatches, and blue jays that wintered over.

Goldfinches roller-coaster through the air toward the backyard feeder. Some have visited the feeder all winter; others have just arrived after the long, hard flight up from the Gulf Coast. Male redwing blackbirds perch in solitary song on rocking reeds in Hockomock Swamp in Easton, Massachusetts. A northern oriole chirps from the lower branch of a maple tree in Bellows Falls, Vermont. In an oak tree beside Route 84 in Hartford, Connecticut, a wood thrush up from Mexico sounds the melodious *pit-pit-pit* familiar to early risers.

A chubby-cheeked indigo bunting recently arrived from the West Indies rests in a willow tree beside the

Connecticut River. A ragged-crested kingfisher keeps a wary eye out for schools of minnow from a lightpost overlooking Dorchester Bay.

Like a swept-winged fighter jet, a barn swallow patrols the air over the Pawtucket River in search of mosquitoes and other delectable morsels. The swallow winters in Argentina. Unlike other birds, it migrates during the day, sometimes traveling as many as 600 miles in 24 hours, eating insects on the wing.

A robin bobs across the lawn in search of dried grass for its nest. Though the robin's arrival is considered a sign of spring, the odds are that it didn't migrate but spent the winter in a swamp or stand of cedars, unseen by car-bound suburbanites.

When the water recedes after the full moon—the Planting Moon, according to the Mohawks, who planted their corn when the leaves of the oak tree were as big as a squirrel's ear—thousands of spike-tailed horseshoe crabs come ashore and congregate on the sand flats of Pleasant Bay on Cape Cod, where they'll meet and mate in a seasonal ritual they've practiced for 200 million years. Armored body parts click and clatter as the crabs drag their tails across the sand to answer the biological imperative on land that won't be flooded again until the next full moon.

In simpler times, fishermen met the horseshoe crabs with clubs and dispatched them in retaliation for their predation on shellfish. Now, the crabs are met by shorebirds that feast on the crab eggs and by technicians, who draw some of their pastel blue blood and return them to the sea unharmed. The crabs' blood contains an anti-infective agent that will be processed into a liquid worth about $15,000 an ounce to the pharmaceutical industry.

As the horseshoe crabs lumber out of the surf on Cape Cod, blooms of insects and algae transform a pond off Beaver Brook in Hollis, New Hampshire, into a jungle. Like creatures from a horror movie, lizardlike newts with bloated bellies float on the pond's surface and submerge with a whip of their tails to pick off tadpoles grazing on the algae below. The algae also provides food for a mallard duck that has chosen the pond to raise its young. A trout feeds on a surface skimmer and makes a half-hearted charge at a frog. The frog escapes but is eventually picked off by a long-legged great blue heron feeding in the shallows at dusk, just as the beavers emerge from their den to continue their assault on a maple tree.

Rattlesnakes take advantage of the delicious spring weather to sun themselves on rock ledges near their ancestral dens in the Blue Hills. Reinvigorated by the sun after their long winter nap, the cold-blooded stalkers continue their search for food—mainly mice, which the snakes locate with infrared sensors on their pointed snouts.

Early colonists with thick sticks and stout hearts discovered that the easiest way to keep rattlers out of their fields was to make a preemptive strike in May. In a holiday mood, the colonists hiked into the Blue Hills and clubbed the reptiles to death as they sunned themselves. A bounty was paid for each dead snake. In Dorchester in 1785, the bounty was one shilling sixpence, about the price of a quart of rum.

There's no bounty on the tent caterpillars that chew their way out of their eggshells and congregate on the trees bordering a pasture in Litchfield, Connecticut, where the caterpillars spin their silk and build communal shelters. Their "tents" are often confused with the webs of the fall webworms, but it's easy to tell the difference: fall webworm shelters are constructed on the ends of branches and surround the leaves on which the caterpillars (webworms) feed. Eastern tent caterpillars build their shelters in the forks of branches, often near the trunk.

It sometimes gets so cold on a New England spring day that the caterpillars can barely move. Their tents create a mini-environment that absorbs sunshine and captures their combined body heat. This warms them up enough that they can set off in search of food. Two or three times a day, the dim-sighted creatures set out in single file to feed. The caterpillars follow established paths marked by scent. Exploratory trails are marked once. Trails that lead to an ample food source are marked again on the way back, creating a scent trail for other caterpillars to follow. A single colony of tent caterpillars can strip a full-grown black cherry tree of all its foliage before the caterpillars pass into nonfeeding pupal and adult stages.

As the sun rises, running water warms up quickly on the days before leaves emerge in the forest and block the sun's light. The warm spring days allow insects and amphibians to begin their brief lives.

On the surface film of a litter-strewn pool outside a culvert in Kittery, Maine, water striders dance and dart at objects on the water and reflections at the bottom of the pool. These long-legged insects feed on other insects and tiny crustaceans. They drill a hole into their victims and suck out their vital juices.

Whirligig beetles also float on the surface as they search for prey. The eyes of these rotund, half-inch-long beetles are divided into two parts. One part allows them to keep a lookout for birds and other predators above the water while the other part allows them to look for prey below. At the first sign of trouble, the beetles sink or fly away.

Mosquito larvae nourished by the warm water in a quiet pool in Mystic, Connecticut, are transformed into adults; the females take wing and fly off in search of blood. Transparent-winged mayflies also emerge from their larval stage, but their mission causes us much less trouble.

In a universe in which we measure the distance light can travel in years and the time it takes an Ice Age to retreat in centuries, most mayflies take wing, mate, and die in 24 hours, a life as poetic as it is brief.

A mayfly looks like a large, brownish mosquito with long forelegs and a wiry tail. These ephemeral fliers have been fluttering around for about 300 million years, since the dinosaurs lumbered over the ferns on which they perched.

Mayflies spend all but the last day of their brief lives as nymphs, infinitesimal, bulbous-eyed creatures with a lobsterlike segmented tail, preying on plankton in local streams and ponds. One day in May, the immature nymphs leave their burrows at the bottoms of ponds and streams and swim up toward the light. As they break through the surface, their skin splits and their wings emerge. The sub-adults rest on the surface film until their wings harden, then fly to shore, where they rest until sundown and molt into adults. At dusk, adult males hover near shore in large mating swarms that fly as high as the treetops. Females soon fly into the swarm and are quickly seized. The mayflies mate on the wing and slowly drop downward until the male breaks off and returns to the swarm. As the moon rises and dark descends, the males land and die, while the females drop to the water's surface in a frantic race to lay eggs before death (perhaps in the form of a hungry trout) happens by. Any survivors fly off and die. Robins, bullfrogs, and dragonflies congregate near the pond or stream to gorge on the love-crazed insects.

May sunshine encourages pine and maple seedlings to burst from the forest floor in what's left of the Great North Woods. The Northeast Forest once stretched from horizon to horizon. Broad-trunked trees were common before the farmers arrived, but soon the old-growth forest was chopped and burned until there wasn't a good stand of pine trees left between Boston and the White Mountains. The flocks of passenger pigeons that once darkened the skies were hunted to extinction. Timber wolves and cougars no longer skulked in the forest. Deer became difficult to find.

Then came the Industrial Revolution. Farmers gave up the dream of prizing a living from the earth during the short New England growing season and turned to the mills of Lowell, Lawrence, and Nashua for their livelihoods. The less impressive, second-growth forest reclaimed the farmland. Stone walls were left behind in silent woods. Lumbering moose returned to the forest. Beavers returned to the streams. There are now more deer than ever, and there have been unconfirmed reports that cougars and timber wolves have returned to the North Country.

May 1

May Day. The midway point between the Spring Equinox and the Summer Solstice. Pagans in Europe celebrated the spring planting and the beginning of the new year today. They built colorful, ribbon-draped maypoles and sang and cavorted around them to ensure a good harvest. Thomas Morton set up a pole in Quincy in 1627. The Puritans sent the reveler into exile.

May 2

An oak seedling rises from an acorn buried by a squirrel last fall. The gregarious rodents hide nuts for later use and often forget where they hid them. Some naturalists believe squirrels were responsible for the return of the trees to the area after the last Ice Age, spreading the seeds northward a couple of hundred yards farther each year from the South, where the seeds had remained untouched by ice.

May 3

Purple and white violets blossom in the shade of a maple tree in Putney, Vermont. Ants collect violet seeds and bury

Rat snake

them in their tunnels. Later, they eat the seed coats, which stimulates the seeds to germinate. Since ants abandon their burrows every four or five weeks, seed buildup isn't a problem; it reduces competition among the germinating flowers.

May 4

A northern walkingstick, three inches long, stands motionless on an oak tree in Waterville, Maine. Superbly camouflaged, this brown, twiglike insect remains inactive during the day. It eats leaves and plant juices at night.

May 5

Terns come in from the ocean to build their nests, little more than shallow scrapes in the sand, on Race Point on Cape Cod. The birds appear to be in no rush to come ashore and lay their eggs. They sometimes sit on debris off the coast, perhaps getting up the nerve to brave the offroad vehicles on shore.

May 6

Under the porch, a blessed event: a skunk gives birth. In a couple of months, mom will bring the kids out hunting. But we rarely see them, since they do most of their prowling at night.

May 7

On a puddingstone out-cropping at the edge of a clearing in Dorchester, Massachusetts, a four-foot rat snake appears coiled and ready to strike. Look closely and you can see the oily glow of its black skin and the angled belly scales that allow it to climb trees. But its flinty eyes are not looking for prey. The snake is dead. Its last meal was a poisoned rat.

May 8

Raucous herring gulls build nests of straw and dried seaweed on islands in Portland Harbor. Larger, black-backed gulls—the bullies on the beach—sometimes take over the herring gulls' nests.

May 9

In 1977, a record May snow fell. The snow was only a half-inch deep in Boston, but 10 inches fell in the suburbs, and 10 to 20 inches accumulated farther inland. There was a lot of damage to trees. The snow melted quickly, but what a surprise!

Night-heron

May 10

Male fiddler crabs scuttle around in salt marshes, waving their one giant claw aggressively. The claw, which gave the crab its name, is part of the male's sexual display. Males fight each other; the one with the bigger claw usually wins.

May 11

Chipmunks skitter into the sunshine, free at last of the dens in which they spent the winter.

May 12

At sunset, black-crowned night-herons take flight from their nesting rookeries in coastal marshes. Stocky, short-necked birds with a black crown and gray wings, they fly sedately up rivers to feed. Night-herons have established feeding territories on the Mystic, Charles, and Neponset Rivers. As the bird's name implies, it's nocturnal. It spends the day roosting in trees or reed beds. You're most likely to hear its distinctive call—a harsh, barking *qwawk*—at night or at dusk.

May 13

Out in a meadow, a turtle stomps its feet. Earthworms below ground think it's raining and flee to the surface to escape drowning, only to be scarfed up by the armorclad con man.

May 14

A hognose snake rears up, flattens its head like a cobra, and shakes its tail menacingly at the edge of the scrub brush under the high power lines in Montpelier, Vermont. Don't let the theatrics fool you; this snake almost never bites. If the ferocious-looking display doesn't send you on your way, the snake will roll over and play dead.

May 15

On this date in 1954, 5.74 inches of rain, a record, fell on Boston in 24 hours.

May 16

Dandelions push up relentlessly through the lawn. Dandelion roots, peeled and sliced like carrots and boiled until soft, kept many an immigrant from starving. When Yankees saw mill workers collecting the weeds in pastures along the Merrimack River in Lowell during the Industrial Revolution, they thought the workers were crazy.

May 17

May sunshine, more intense than in August because of the advantageous tilt of the Earth, brings garter snakes out of their burrows to warm themselves. These ubiquitous reptiles don't lay eggs. Their young are born alive, a survival strategy that allows garter snakes to survive in suburbia because they don't have to leave eggs in nesting sites, where skunks and raccoons can prey on them.

May 18

Pink lady's slippers, or moccasin-flowers, blossom on the pine forest floor. This bulbous-pouched flower has a slit down its front that small insects can't pry open. Bumblebees are strong enough to penetrate it, though. After the bumblebee enters, it finds its only exit is up through the throat of the flower. The bee becomes painted with pollen as it struggles through the tiny opening.

May 19

On this date in 1780, near-total darkness descended on New England. Candles were lit. Birds went home to roost. Some thought the day of judgment was at hand. It wasn't, but no scientific cause for the darkness was ever determined. In Connecticut, they call May 19 "Dark Day"; a bicentennial observance was held in 1980. John Greenleaf Whittier wrote a poem about the 1780 event, even though he was born 27 later.

May 20

Hordes of shorebirds pour up the coast: plovers, sandpipers, red knots—marvelous flyers, all of them.

May 21

Delicate white and tan *champignon* mushrooms create dark circles on untreated lawns. The ancients called them fairy rings and thought the circles were magical places. A fairy ring beside a house was said to bring good luck, though harm might come to a cow that fed inside the circle. It was thought that you would become enchanted if you entered the fairy ring during a full moon. Love potions were made of dew collected there.

May 22

Fifty-ton humpback whales are out on Stellwagen Bank, feeding on the spring plankton bloom and the small fish it attracts. In warmer waters they sometimes form a large circle and blow a wall of bubbles. Fish trapped inside the ring swim to the surface, where other members of the pod of humpbacks eat them. Scientists call this "bubble-net feeding." It's been seen off Cape Cod once or twice.

May 23

The trumpet-blossomed purple trillium blooms on the forest floor in the Berkshires. The flower is noted more for its unpleasant smell than its beauty. Swamp Yankees called it "stinking Benjamin." Woodsmen called the plant "Indian balm"; Native Americans used the dried underground stems to hasten childbirth; they also used it to treat snakebite.

May 24

Bullfrogs in local swamps croak their *chug-a-rumph*. The males, chunky amphibians nearly five inches long—the largest frogs in New England—are advertising themselves to females. The bigger the voice, the more attractive the frog. The females lay a gelatinous mass of eggs in the shallows. The eggs are sometimes eaten by their parents, who barely recognize them.

May 25

A male ruffed grouse—a brown, chickenlike bird with a fan-shaped, black-banded tail—sashays into a light-dappled thicket in the Green Mountains of Vermont. Male grouse don't sing to attract mates. Instead, they mount a favorite log, puff up their feathers, beat their wings until they blur, and make a loud drumming noise. To some observers, it sounds like a power saw starting.

May 26

The temperature reached a record high on this date in 1880, when it was 97 degrees in Boston.

May 27

As you turn over the dirt in the garden, the loam is rich with finger-thick grubs. They morph into June bugs, which will slam into outdoor lights next month.

May 28

The exotic Dutchman's-breeches blossoms in the forest in Framingham, Massachusetts. This spring ephemeral takes advantage of the ample sunlight before the leaves block out the sun. Its delicate cream-colored flowers suggest elfin breeches hanging out to dry.

May 29

Ruby-throated hummingbirds begin to arrive in the backyard, up from their wintering grounds in Central America. These tiny birds weigh barely one-tenth of an ounce and can't glide, so they make the entire trip north under full power. Some fly 600 miles nonstop over the Gulf of Mexico; others take the inland route.

May 30

A chimney swift finds shelter for the night in a chimney in Dracut, Massachusetts. Before the Europeans arrived, the birds sought shelter in big hollow trees. When tree cavities became scarce after most of the large trees were decimated, the swifts began seeking shelter in chimneys. The birds build their nests in chimneys, too.

May 31

Traditional day for the first appearance of the

aggressive, infinitesimal blackflies in the northern woods. Clouds of the voracious vampires end their larval aquatic phase and ride bubbles to the surface, where the females take wing in search of blood to nurture their eggs. Blackflies were the bane of the early settlers, who didn't have insect repellent. Native Americans slathered their bodies with animal fat to ward off the biting insets. The smell convinced some settlers that the natives were savages.

Humpback whales

With the bitter winter behind us and a stifling summer to come, June is the month when wildlife is most active in New England. From the seaweed-draped granite ledges of Maine to the ice-crusted cracks of Tuckerman Ravine on Mount Washington, creatures are stirring. But many animals go about their business sight unseen, making their rounds under cover of darkness.

Brown bats knife through the night air, catching mosquitoes on the wing over a dairy farm in Pomfret, Connecticut. A surly raccoon lumbers through the shadows in Hartford, searching for anything remotely edible, and snarls at a housecat. Moths flutter around porch lights in Roxbury while a nighthawk the size of a robin performs aerial acrobatics over Fenway Park. A coyote skulks out of the

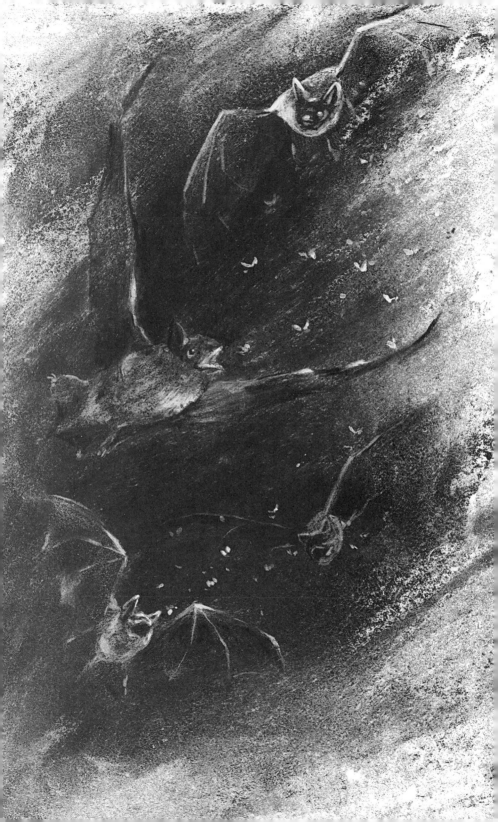

range of headlights as it searches the side of Route 93 for a tasty roadkill. A skunk raises a ruckus as it bulls though the bushes of Nashua. One of the noisiest creatures, it wants you to see it; its best defense is recognition. On a tributary of the Saco River, a beaver patrols its self-made pond, making sure all is in order before beginning its night's work. Lightning bugs blink in the backyard, signaling their availability for amorous adventures. The squawk and chatter of hundreds of songbirds announce impending dawn, even in East Boston, where house sparrows and finches live out their lives at rooftop level.

A June bug big as a thumbnail crunches into a screen door. A mosquito drills into the forearm of an unsuspecting gardener. Fireflies scratch the darkness near a lilac bush, while clouds of newly hatched blackflies congregate over a streambed. A brown spider spins its web in a corner of the garage. Earthworms once again go about their subterranean business, though they slither to the surface after a rainfall to escape drowning.

Though it's hard to imagine, invertebrates—mostly insects and spiders but other soft-bodied organisms without backbones as well—account for 90 to 95 percent of our animal species and a similar proportion of the total animal weight on Earth. Some experts have estimated that the collective weight of these creatures is 55 times greater than that of all the humans on Earth.

After a winter of dormancy, insects and other invertebrates once again rule the Earth.

Pesky saw-mouthed mosquitoes patrol the night in search of blood. Less than 5 percent of human skin contains blood vessels, so the mosquitoes have to probe for their meals, sawing through tissue in search of paydirt. When a mosquito does hit blood, she pumps spitballs of vessel dilators and blood thinners into your body to keep the blood running freely. An allergic reaction to mosquito drool is what produces those itchy red lumps.

About 150 species of mosquitoes make the United States their home, but not all bite people. Some mosquitoes prefer frogs, snakes, and other cold-blooded animals. Others prey primarily on birds.

Only female mosquitoes bite. They need a victim's blood for the development of eggs inside their bodies. Female mosquitoes are voracious insects; they draw up to three times their body weight in blood and can barely fly away to digest their meals. Males feed exclusively on nectar. The insect's distinctive buzz is made by its wings, which move about 1,000 times a second. The females' wings make a higher-pitched tone than the males', which helps the mosquitoes find mates.

These little flies (*mosquito* means "little fly" in Spanish) hear and smell through two antennae in the centers of their heads. Two huge compound eyes cover most of their heads. Each lens points in a different direction and works independently, so a mosquito cannot focus its eyes for sharp vision, but it can detect movement quickly.

Mosquitoes find their prey mainly by smell. Carbon dioxide, exhaled in our breath and given off in other body vapors, leads them to humans. Mosquitoes can detect a plume of carbon dioxide from 50 feet away. They can also sense the lactic acid that exudes from our hands, faces, and shoulders. Some people excrete more lactic acid than others. That is why some of us get bitten more often than others.

Insect repellents do not repel the pests; they merely mask human odors so the fuzzy-visioned insects can't recognize a good meal when they smell one.

The weather has become warm enough for turtles to become active on College Pond in Plymouth, Massachusetts. The armored reptiles are dependent on sunlight to warm their bodies. They often pass through backyards in their single-minded pursuit of insects, worms, and berries. As a turtle lumbers across the yard on bowed legs, barely able to drag its shell across the lawn, it looks like a visitor from another planet, and in a way, it is: turtles first appeared about 250 million years ago, when dinosaurs still roamed the area.

Common backyard visitors are box turtles with yellow and orange splotches of color on their black shells. The undershell, or plastron, is hinged a third of the way back from the turtle's head, enabling it to draw itself into a shell and close it like a lid, hence the name "box turtle."

Native Americans predicted weather by turtles' behavior: if the turtles stayed in their shells, dry weather was to be expected; if they remained active, rain was on tap. Some Indian nations even called America "Turtle Island."

Turtles are North America's longest-lived reptile. They have been known to roam the Earth for more than 138 years. So keep in mind that your backyard visitor may have made its last pass through the area during the Civil War.

Some animals thrive in the presence of man. Deer, which feed on the tender bark and leaves of small trees and shrubs growing on the border between forest and clearing, adapt well to suburbia. Experts estimate that more of these silent herbivores now live in New England than did before the Europeans "discovered" the New World.

There are more raccoons and skunks in the suburbs than there are in the woods. Unsecured trash bags provide them with a daily buffet. The black bear population is booming, too. Black bears are beginning to appear in the suburbs, as are some moose, following the roughage under high power lines down from the north.

Swept-winged peregrine falcons, once almost extirpated by DDT in the food chain, have returned to set up housekeeping on tall buildings in

Boston and Manchester, New Hampshire, where the vertical structures with ledges offer all the advantages of the cliffsides they once nested on.

The elimination of DDT has also reinvigorated life on a beaver pond on a tributary of the Merrimack River. At dawn, a deer emerges from the water and shakes itself off, shedding water that sparkles like silver in the oblique sunlight. The bulbous eyes of a newt break the surface of the pond as it dog-paddles like a tiny water dragon. Three neon dragonflies dart over the water while a barn swallow sweeps through the air in search of mosquitoes to fill its plump white belly. An American copper butterfly, orange and gray with black dots, dabbles over a yellow flag iris on the bank of the pond while a school of squirmy tadpoles circles in its shadow. At night, the bassy *jug-o'-rum* of bullfrogs and trill of peepers punctuate the silence.

Later, as the Hay Moon rises and dances over the rippling water, the *hoo-hoo-hoot* of an owl is heard as it stakes out its hunting territory.

In the shadowy hollow along the pond bank, fireflies etch the night with fire. A special enzyme called luciferin enables them to create the light that they use to send flashing, coded messages to attract a mate.

Fireflies have delighted watchers for centuries. They were first reported in a Chinese manuscript written about 2000 B.C. According to some reports, in 1519, during Cortez's conquest of Mexico, his small band surrounded a much larger force of Indians in the Aztec town of Cempoala in Veracruz. The besieged natives saw the light of thousands of fireflies around them, assumed them to be matches poised at the breeches of muskets of a vast army, and surrendered.

Even today, the flashing of fireflies can lead to miscommunication. Most species of firefly create a toxin that makes them unappetizing to hungry birds. But the *Photuris* firefly does not. When the female *Photuris* emerges from its cocoon, it is at the mercy of predators such as spiders and birds. But it can acquire the protective toxin it needs by feeding regularly on the male *Photinus* firefly. When the male *Photinus* uses its light to locate a receptive female, the *Photinus* female sends the appropriate response. When the lusty insect arrives, she devours it, acquiring a supply of the defensive toxin for herself.

Before the beaver got there, this pond didn't exist. It is now home to a number of different species. When the beaver dies or moves on, the dam will decay and the pond will drain, leaving behind a meadow and a home for a whole new cast of critters.

June 1

An ambush bug, white and yellow with a hint of green, is perfectly camouflaged as it sits on a rhododendron leaf in Newport, Rhode Island. When an unwitting honeybee alights, the bug inserts its hollow beak into the bee and injects enzymes that make soup and an easy meal of the luckless insect.

June 2

A snowy egret stalks minnows in the shallows of the Neponset River. The long-legged waders are making a comeback. They were slaughtered to near extinction for their snazzy plumes by the Victorian hat trade.

June 3

Down in the damp, dark cellar, a silverfish slithers across a moldy stack of newspapers. The creepy, crawly multilegged insect is one of the few animals that can digest paper.

June 4

To the surprise of a Cantabrigian, a blue jay screeches into the grass and rises with a mouse. Twenty-five percent of the bird's food is animal: bugs, salamanders, tree frogs, and even mice.

June 5

A duckling peeps in alarm when it becomes separated from its mother on a salt marsh in Eastham. But Mom isn't the only one listening. A V-winged harrier, or "marsh hawk," swoops down and makes short work of the disoriented duckling.

June 6

Honey locust is in bloom. The hanging white flowers resemble thick lilac blossoms, but the smell is sweeter.

June 7

Male dragonflies begin to set up exclusive mating territories over local swamps. The transparent-winged predators are very

Snowy egret

aggressive. They keep a bulbous eye out for competitors as they relentlessly crisscross their territory, catching insects on the wing.

June 8

In Houghton's Pond in Canton, Massachusetts, a pumpkinseed sunfish methodically mouths a bullrush in search of damselfly nymphs.

June 9

Tornadoes are rare in New England. They require too many things to happen at once: warm air on the surface, cold air aloft, and some rotation in the cloud system to pull the air into a vortex. On this day in 1953, the conditions all came together in a Worcester tornado that killed 85 and injured 1,288 people. It caused $10 million in damage.

June 10

A female snapping turtle lumbers out of the water in Carver, Massachusetts, and scratches out a shallow nest in the sand, where she deposits 20 leathery eggs. No nurturing mother, this will be the last she sees of her offspring.

June 11

A "nightingale" calls in the middle of the night in Greenwich, Connecticut. Real nightingales live in England. Around here, the midnight serenader is usually a mockingbird, which will sometimes sing all night.

June 12

As the ocean warms, sand lances, also called sand eels, teem in offshore waters. They're a favorite of the humpback whales now summering on Stellwagen Bank off Cape Cod.

June 13

A green frog calls from a swamp in Peterborough, New Hampshire. Its call sounds like a breaking banjo string. This jumpy amphibian is not wary; if cornered, it inflates its body and stands tall.

June 14

Periwinkles, the small brown snails, have moved into the shallows of the Ducktrap Inlet in Lincolnville, Maine, for mating. Periwinkles are preyed on by moon snails, which attach themselves to the periwinkle and exude a mild acid that softens the victim's shell. This allows the moon snail to get at the body inside the shell with its hard, rasping tongue.

Moon snail and periwinkle

June 15

An ant invades a termite colony in New Haven, Connecticut, and insect alarm bells go off. With a sharp contraction of its abdomen, a termite explodes, covering the invader with a viscous mass of internal organs and blood—the dooms-day defense.

June 16

A cat scrambles up a tree after a squirrel and soon faces a dilemma. The squirrel has opposable claws that allow it to climb up and down. The cat has claws on the front of its paws, a design that assists the cat only in climbing up. The cat gingerly backs down, looking more like prey than predator as it clumsily slides down the trunk.

June 17

An eastern hare with ears as big as a donkey's munches on tender grass in a clearing in the White Mountains of New Hampshire. Early European settlers considered hares bad luck. The settlers thought witches transformed themselves into the big bunnies.

June 18

A killing frost on this date in 1816 blackened leaves on trees throughout New England. The cold was the result of soot spewed into the atmosphere by the eruption of Mount Tambora in Bali.

June 19

Carnivorous pitcher plants blossom in a bush-lined bog in Carver, Massachusetts. Their blossom forms a cup-shaped trap with slippery sides where insects drown and decompose. The insects provide nutrients the plant might not otherwise get in the sphagnum bogs where it grows, which are almost sterile.

June 20

Wild irises blossom at the edge of local swamps: two species grow there—the blue flag and the yellow flag.

June 21

The Summer Solstice, our longest day, with 15 hours of daylight. The word *solstice* means "sun stands still." The Summer Solstice was a big event for our agrarian ancestors. It is one of the "lesser sabbats" of the Wiccan religion. Druids, the Egyptians, and other nature worshippers also celebrated the sun, our nearest star.

June 22

With a plop, a sharp-snouted northern water shrew dives into Silver Lake in Hollis, New Hampshire, and hurtles after a fingerling trout. In a flash, it's over, and the mouselike mammal swims toward the surface with its wriggling prey. This prodigious three-ounce predator feeds almost continuously.

June 23

With a slap that can be heard for a quarter-mile around its pond in the foothills near Stinson Lake in New Hampshire, a beaver splashes its tail to warn its family of danger. It's 3 A.M. and the beavers are working on their twig-stiffened dam by moonlight.

June 24

A female wasp seizes and stings an unsuspecting housefly dawdling over a hamburger wrapper discarded at the edge of a McDonald's parking lot. Paralyzed but not dead, the fly will still be fresh when it's fed to the larvae in the wasp's paper nest.

June 25

Baby birds are up on unsteady wings and anxious parents are particularly vocal. Mockingbirds are the most irascible; they'll chase off cats.

June 26

A fisher spider stalks the waters of Jamaica Pond. This arachnid doesn't spin a web to trap its victims; it rests on a water lily pad with one or two feet in the water, where it can detect ripples created by insects trapped on the surface film. After retrieving an insect, the spider then follows a lifeline of silk back to the lily pad, where it devours its prey. This spider will catch small fish, too, by dabbling one leg in the water as a lure.

June 27

Moon jellyfish float into the shallows near Gloucester Harbor to breed. The four distinctive white circles in the center of their gelatinous bodies is part of their reproductive apparatus. These jellyfish are eaten by leatherback turtles and

Wasp and housefly

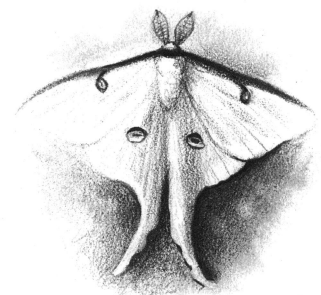

Luna moth

are sometimes stranded on the shore by low tide, where they die in the sunshine.

June 28

A luna moth as big as a baby's fist hovers around a streetlight in Holyoke, Massachusetts. The green moth with the eyespots on its wings has just emerged from its cocoon. The adult moth has no mouth and will not eat during the four or five days in which it will fly, mate, lay eggs, and die.

June 29

At dusk in the second-growth forest in Bow, New Hampshire, a male pileated woodpecker, or "logcock," warms a clutch of eggs in a hollow tree cavity. The female departs to roost in another hole in a distant tree, leaving the male in charge of the eggs for the night. The birds mate for life and the male spends most of the time on the nest. These large woodpeckers are shy of humans and are rarely seen, but you might spot one of their rectangular excavations in a tree.

June 30

Time warp. Today's the day we add or subtract a second to reconcile the atomic clock and astronomical time. It's up to the clock watchers in the Bureau International de l'Heure in Paris to decide.

A QUICKSILVER SCHOOL OF MENHADEN SKITTERS along the surface of a small inlet on Portsmouth Harbor and arcs along the shoreline, roiling the surface of the water. One fish leaps out of the water onto the rocks. Another fish leaps out, and another and another.

It's July and the bluefish are back from their wintering grounds off South Florida. This school of blues has trapped the foot-long menhaden in the shallows. The water soon turns red with blood.

Gulls soar over the inlet, waiting for leftovers. They won't get in the water; it's too dangerous. Blues are voracious feeders and will bite anything in their paths. They injure as many fish as they eat with their needle-sharp teeth. Bluefish often bite each other in their feeding frenzy.

It has been estimated that bluefish kill well over 1 billion fish off New England during their annual summer visit.

Blues are not large fish—the biggest one on record (caught off Nantucket in 1903) measured 3 feet, 9 inches long and weighed 27 pounds—but they travel in great schools. In 1965, a commercial fisherman found a school off Martha's Vineyard that was 35 miles across.

On Rye Beach, New Hampshire, half-naked sunbathers basted with coconut butter invade the intertidal zone, the prized land between the points of high and low tides, where many organisms rely on the water to keep them wet, to bring in food, and to remove waste products. A laughing gull cries hysterically as it glides over the high-tide line marked by knotted wrack, an olive-colored algae with knots, or air bladders, that fragrantly decays in the sun. A piece of driftwood entangled in the seaweed is riddled with the tunnels of common shipworms—long, slender clams that ruined many a boat during the days of sail. The leathery dried black pouch with four horns decaying on the sand is called a mermaid's purse. It's the egg case of a skate. The dead starfish with the orange spot is a *Forbes asterias*. Starfish prey on clams by pulling apart their shells with hundreds of suction-tube feet and sliding their stomachs inside the shell to digest the contents. The sun-baked shell of a surf clam has a BB-sized hole in it where a northern moon shell snail drilled a hole to feast on the clam inside. Beach fleas, which are actually tiny crustaceans that look like pale fleas, hop into the air at the approach of footfalls and burrow into the sand.

Inland, in an abandoned, weed-choked pasture beside Route 95, the monarch butterfly and the milkweed plant perform a remarkable pas de deux. The orange butterfly with the black piping and the plant with the silk stuffing have developed an unusual relationship. The nectar of the milkweed plant is toxic. The monarch butterfly, the plant's prime pollinator, has adapted to that poison.

The toxin concentrates in the butterfly's wings, where it can do the most damage to a predator foolish enough to take a bite. An immature blue jay may occasionally grab a mouthful by mistake. The poison results in gastric distress rather than death. For the most part, however, the butterfly's bright colors successfully warn hungry predators to look elsewhere for lunch.

The viceroy butterfly has taken a different evolutionary tack—its coloration mimics that of the monarch. Even without the poison, the ploy works. The bright colors warn predators away from the viceroy as well.

But this survival technique has a drawback for the monarch: a parasitic fly (*Zenillia adamsoni*) is resistant to the monarch's poison. When the female fly is ready to lay her eggs, she seeks out a monarch caterpillar and deposits her eggs on it. When the eggs hatch, the fly larvae bore into the caterpillar and consumes it from within. The fly offspring then carry a supply of the poison that protects them, too.

In the shade at the edge of the pasture, the fruit of a wild strawberry turns white before ripening, alerting birds to its impending availability, during this, the month of the Strawberry Moon. Native Americans dried the fruit and pounded it into "leather," which they saved for the winter. Starving colonial Minutemen avoided scurvy by drinking a tea made from the plant's leaves.

The crack and rumble of thunder become familiar sounds in the Merrimack Valley as July's hot, humid days give birth to some of the region's most dramatic weather.

At dawn, the sun rises over a clear sky and the ground begins to heat up. Because the warm air is lighter than cool air, the warm air rises, expands, and becomes colder. Water vapor in the air creates small cumulus clouds. As the cumulus clouds continue to grow, some spread out at the top, forming an anvilshape, and extend ahead of the main clouds. A thunderstorm is about to be born, one of 50,000 that will affect the world today.

The tops of the clouds rise as high as 70,000 feet, where the temperature is well below freezing. Inside the clouds, air currents move up and down as fast as 5,000 feet per minute. The water vapor condenses rapidly, resulting in a heavy downpour that grabs the attention of valley dwellers.

The motion of the air causes electrical charges to build up in the clouds. These charges produce lightning. When the lightning flashes, it heats the air around it. The air expands violently and creates the rumble of thunder that sends valley dwellers scrambling for cover.

Deep, rumbling thunder is created by lightning that is a good distance away. Crackling thunder is closer. The clap of thunder reaches the ear after the lightning has struck, because light travels faster than sound. Count the seconds between the lightning flash and the sound of thunder, divide by five, and you've determined how many miles away the lightning struck. Massachusetts has the most thunderstorms in the month of July, about five.

The eerie wail of a coyote. The insistent *hoo-hoo-hoot* of an owl. The chilling crunch of footfalls through dry leaves in the dark. A nighttime walk in the woods can be unnerving. But if you immerse yourself in the experience and become at one with the woods, there's a lot to recommend it. Raccoons, skunks, and foxes are active at night, along with snakes and other animals that don't like the heat of the day. Rabbits and deer are also about, as are some spiders, whose beady eyes glow red in the dark. You might even come across a bed of bladder campion, a tiny, star-shaped flower that blossoms at night and is pollinated by moths.

In July, tourist traffic peaks on Mount Washington in New Hampshire. The Cog Railway belches black soot into the crystalline mountain air, cars snake up the Auto Road, and hikers sweat and grumble toward the summit of the 6,288-foot peak. Every thousand feet they gain in altitude is the ecological equivalent of traveling a climate zone north—or several thousand years into the past.

At the foot of the mountain stand the familiar maple and beech trees. At higher elevations, these hardwoods yield to more hardy birches, which in turn give way to red spruce and balsam. At about 4,800 feet, these evergreens become gnarled and twisted into a mat of *krummholz*, or crooked wood. These trees may be more than 100 years old, but they are rarely more than 12 inches tall, their size dictated by the relentless winds and wind-driven ice. Above tree line, at about 5,800 feet, the harsh climate nourishes only lichen, moss, and other simple plants that get most of their moisture from the cold fog. This forbidding, nearly plantless moonscape looks much like Greater Boston did 12,000 years ago, when the last Ice Age retreated.

A light wind off the water cools sunbathers on West Dennis Beach on Cape Cod. When hot air rising over land is replaced by cooler air blowing in from the water, a sea breeze is created. The body of water need not be large. The Charles River sometimes creates a "sea breeze" that can be felt only a block away. On south-facing coastal areas such as Dennis, southwest winds increase the sea-breeze effect.

July 1

A beaver strips the bark of a maple tree in a pond in Hamilton, Massachusetts. In 1932, a colony appeared on a brook in West Stockbridge, presumably after immigrating from New York. There are now about 40,000 in the Bay State. Beavers were extirpated in the state by the late 1800s.

July 2

An errant thousand-pound leatherback turtle swims north to the Gulf of Maine with measured strokes. The largest turtle, the leatherback got its name from its slightly flexible, rubbery shell. They eat jellyfish and an occasional crab.

July 3

The beginning of the dog days of summer, which ends August 11. The ancients believed this to be an evil time when the sea boiled, wine turned sour, and dogs grew mad. They sacrificed a dog to appease the rage of the dog star. Sirius in the constellation Canis Major is the brightest star in the night sky. Ancient Egyptians named it the "dog star" after their god Osiris, whose head resembles a dog's. The Egyptians believed that the light of Sirius contributed to the summer heat.

July 4

Wild blueberries begin to ripen on south-facing hillsides in the Berkshires. Black bears enjoy the fruit as much as we do. They often bring their cubs out for a midafternoon munch out on rocky patches in the foothills of the White Mountains.

July 5

Butter-and-eggs blossom along roads and pastures. These colorful weeds are nearly as common as dandelions, except they don't grow on lawns. The two-foot-tall plants have linear green leaves and clusters of pale yellow flowers with two-lobed lips; the lower lip has an orange "yolk."

Beaver

July 6

A chubby, black and green dogday cicada or harvest-fly—one inch long, with bulbous eyes and fold-back wings—emits the loud buzz-saw sound so familiar in summer. Only the male emits the call, using drumlike membranes on the sides of its abdomen. The buzz is a mating call—the louder, the better. After mating, the female cicada will deposit as many as 600 eggs on a tree trunk. Wingless nymphs hatch, drop, and burrow into the ground, where they will spend the next several years living off the sap of tree roots until they emerge for their final brief fling as an adult.

July 7

Goldfinches twitter exuberantly in an overgrown hayfield as the cars hurtle by on Route 95 in Stratford, Connecticut. They're the last birds to start nesting. Goldfinches like to line their nests with the softest thistle down; they have to wait for the thistle to flower and go to seed before they can build a nest that suits them.

July 8

In the high grass behind an abandoned gas station in Lawrence, Massachusetts, a blessed event occurs: a mouselike meadow vole gives birth. Meadow voles breed all year round and produce up to 17 litters, each with 6 to 10 young. Their population is kept under control by a large number of predators—hawks and owls, blue jays, crows, gulls, herons, cats, raccoons, foxes, skunks, opossums, even bass and other fish.

July 9

On this date in 1816 ("eighteen hundred and froze to death"), the famed year without a summer, frost killed the New England corn crop and some ice still remained on lakes in Canada. The unusual weather was the result of ash spewed into the atmosphere by Mount Tambora in Bali the year before, but nobody knew it at the time. Some suspected unearthly intervention.

July 10

A carpenter bee almost as big as a bumblebee, metallic blue-black with green and purplish streaks, burrows into punky wood in the garage to lay its eggs.

July 11

The Asian shore crab is invading local beaches. These crabs are green or purple and have triangular bodies. They feed on anything in their paths, including shellfish seedlings. The invasive crabs first appeared in New Jersey in 1988 and probably arrived in this country in the ballast of a ship.

Black bears

Carpenter bee

July 12

Daddy-long-legs—harmless arachnids that look as if they are walking on long pairs of stilts—often wave one pair of their appendages around in the air ahead of them touching and smelling their way along. English farmers thought these spiderlike creatures looked as if they were reaping, and they named the arachnids "harvestmen." They thought it was bad luck to kill them.

July 13

The well-named blood worm, nearly a foot long, is buried in the muck at low tide on the fragrant clam flat in Bath, Maine. It has a muscular snout armed with four small hooks that can shoot forward to capture prey; the hooks can also pinch the fingers of fishermen who use them for bait. If cut, it has bright red blood.

July 14

Mysterious Indian pipes grow in the shade of a pine tree in Bethlehem, New Hampshire. Totally white and ghostly in appearance, they're 10 inches tall and have waxy, odorless flowers. They grow without chlorophyll, obtaining nourishment from tree roots channeled through fungus. Some think these plants have mystical powers.

July 15

Less well known but just as accurate a weather predictor as Groundhog Day is St. Swithin's Day: "On Swithin's Day, if thee dost rain, for 40 days will remain; St. Swithin's Day, if thee be faire, for 40 days twill rain no maer."

July 16

In the parking lot behind an apartment building in Beverly, Massachusetts, a foot-long snapping turtle with a serious-looking beak rears on it back legs and snaps at a startled motorist. Though the armored intruder appears vicious on land, it is aggressive only because it's out of its element. In the water, this turtle is usually docile and harmless; swimmers need have no fear.

July 17

On Cape Cod, this year's crop of alewives are slipping downstream away from Pilgrim Lake in Orleans and Stony Brook in Brewster out into the Atlantic. They're an inch and a half long now; and the few sea-run fish that survive will be back in three or four years to breed.

July 18

A porcupine lumbers into an abandoned camp in Gilford, New Hampshire, and joins 10 others. Nobody's sure why these solitary animals sometimes flock up in summer. They may be looking for salt.

July 19

Cool out in the shade of a maple in the backyard. Through the heat exchange provided by the evaporation of water on its leaves, a mature tree provides as much cooling power as five 10,000-watt air conditioners.

July 20

Horseflies, commonly known as "greenheads," harass sunbathers at Crane's Beach in Ipswich, Massachusetts. The bite of their razor-sharp mouthparts feels more like a sting. Like mosquitoes, only the female greenheads bite. They use the blood to nourish their eggs. Unlike mosquitoes, these bulbous-eyed insects are visually oriented; you can't fool them with repellent. Pest controllers trap and kill them. In one week a single trap may catch 30,000 of these biting "flies."

July 21

A garden snail inches toward a tomato patch in a well-tended garden in Putney, Vermont. These snails were brought to the New World by early French settlers, who ate them. Garden snails can now be found in most of the United States.

July 22

Red squirrels cackle and chatter when their territory is violated in the pine forest. Unlike gray squirrels, red squirrels are good swimmers. They have been found far out in big lakes like Champlain and Winnipesaukee.

July 23

Flying squirrels are airborne in dark suburban woodlots on warm nights. They're a little smaller than big red squirrels, with gray fur and big black eyes. Flying squirrels glide on flaps of skin that run between the forelimbs and hindquarters on each side of their bodies. They live in the hollow trunks of dead trees.

July 24

On a granite ledge at the sudsy edge of the water in Kittery, Maine, is a common periwinkle, brown with a blunt spire, about 1½ inches long. It's a creature of the tidal line that can survive out of water for long periods of time. It is our most common periwinkle, but it's not a native species. It spread here from Europe, probably hitching a ride on the hull of a ship.

July 25

A diminutive nectar eater, a ruby-throated hummingbird backs up to get a better look at a beach rose bush in front of a cottage in Chatham, on Cape Cod. Hummingbirds are the only birds in the East that can fly backward.

July 26

Glossy-leaved winter-
green provides ground
cover on the forest floor
on Mount Mansfield.
Wintergreen contains
methyl salicylate, a basic
compound similar to
salicylic acid in aspirin.
Native Americans sipped
wintergreen tea to soothe
aching muscles.

Hummingbird

July 27

Migrating south, a solitary
sandpiper flies swiftly
over the ferry terminal in
Rockland, Maine, after its
nesting in the Arctic was
interrupted. This bird is
the vanguard of millions
of shorebirds that will
flow back next month.
Some birds return early
because their eggs were
eaten by an arctic fox,
or their nestlings were
killed by biting insects,
or because of any number
of natural calamities.

July 28

Thumb-sized leopard
frogs, green or brown
with red spots, begin to
leap across the lawn.

They were polliwogs just
a few short weeks ago.

July 29

An olive-green sea urchin
with long blunt spines
scours the ledges off
Vinalhaven, Maine, for
algae. Some call these
prickly globular inverte-
brates the "hedgehogs of
the sea." Sea urchins are
harvested by scuba diver
for the Japanese sushi
market.

July 30

A flounder feeds on the
bottom of Quincy Bay. It
is widely believed that
the majority of fish live
in tropical waters, but
that is a misconception.
Cold water holds more
oxygen than warm, so sea
life becomes more abun-
dant the closer you get to
the poles.

July 31

A hailstorm dropped 12
inches of ice on Scituate,
Massachusetts, in 1769. It
took two days for the ice
to melt.

AUGUST IS THE MONTH THE PERSEID METEOR showers scratch the night with fire as the Earth's upper atmosphere gets sandblasted by the wide, thin river of dust shed thousands of years ago by Comet Swift-Tuttle.

In a good year, you can expect to see about one meteor a minute as the dust particles encounter the Earth's atmosphere about 40 to 80 miles up and meet a fiery death. Some "shooting stars" are visible for only a moment, but others are so bright that they elicit *oohs* and *aahs* as they arc across the sky from zenith to horizon. Meteorites reach the atmosphere at a speed of about 37 miles per second, 80 times faster than a speeding bullet. The Earth encounters the particles head-on, like a car driving into the rain, which is what makes the show so dramatic, as meteorites the consistency of cigarette ash flare into the Earth's atmosphere at 150,000 miles per hour.

In rural Europe, they call them the "tears of St. Lawrence," after the martyr who was allegedly roasted alive. Local folk wisdom says spotting a "shooting star" is good luck, so grab a beach chair and some insect repellent and stretch out on a golf course, a beach, or an isolated stretch of woods away from city lights. Look for them in the northeast sky in the constellation Perseus. Check an almanac for peak viewing nights. Get away from city lights for best viewing.

Under the Sturgeon Moon, purple loosestrife blossoms at the swampy edge of wetlands and drainage ditches along highways from Bridgeport, Connecticut, to Eastport, Maine. The spike-shaped flowers look pretty, but they're pests imported from Eurasia as ornamental flowers. The flowers reproduce relentlessly, squeezing out cattails and other native plants, as well as ducks, geese, and muskrats, which can't use the loosestrife plants for food or cover. Naturalists suggest uprooting the flower if you see it. But it seems much too late for that—loosestrife is everywhere. At least one species loves it, however: honeybees are dancing in their hives.

A honeybee colony consists of about 50,000 individuals. Unlike a town of 50,000 unrelated residents with conflicting values, the honeybees are all related, all children of the same queen, and their one mission in life is the survival of the hive. Purple loosestrife provides a key element in that survival—a steady source of food.

A honeybee scout may cover an area as large as 45 square miles. When a scout returns to the hive after spotting a stand of purple loosestrife or other steady source of nectar, it does a "waggle dance" to communicate the exact location of the plants to its sisters. The scout's dance begins with a straight line and ends with a series of figure-eights. The straight line indicates the direction to and distance of the flowers. Much as we use the top of a map to indicate true north, the scouts use the top of the hive to indicate the direction of the sun.

When purple loosestrife is in bloom, honey production may increase by as much as 25 percent. That's why beekeepers often locate their hives at the edge of wetlands near a stand of these flowers.

Honeybees, like purple loosestrife, are not native to the United States. The bees were introduced by European settlers. First mention of their arrival was in the manifest of a ship that arrived in Jamestown, Virginia, in 1621. They were introduced to New England about the same time.

Colonists used honey as a sweetener when sugar was still a rich man's treat; they used beeswax to make candles, a necessity at the time. Bees were also useful in the pollination of crops, though the procedure was little understood at the time.

Honeybees are social insects that nest in colonies headed by a single fertile female, the queen. The queen is generally the only egg-layer in the colony. The bees are noted for their clustering behavior and for their ability to cool their nests through the evaporation of water collected outside, an ability that allows them to colonize areas unsuitable for other insects.

These small, dark, reddish brown or black bees with orange-yellow rings are familiar to most people, but they are often mistaken for yellow jackets.

Honeybees are thought to have originally appeared on the planet at about the same time as flowering plants, 146 to 74 million years ago, though the oldest bee fossils date from 96 to 74 million years ago. It is thought that they evolved from hunting wasps that acquired a taste for nectar and became vegetarians.

Some of the honeybees escaped the early settlers and colonized hollow trees. It's not unusual to find them in the wild. Native Americans associated them with European settlements and called them the "white man's fly."

August is the peak of the recreational fishing season. Every time a fisherman pulls up a cod, he lays his hands on a wriggling, breathing relic of New England history. It was cod that first brought European visitors to the shores of New England. John Cabot set sail from Bristol, England, on May 2, 1497, with a crew of 18 to "to seke out, discover and finde whatsoever isles, countries, regions or provinces, which before this time have been unknown to all Christians."

On June 24, he "discovered" a "New Founde Land" that might not have held the riches of spices or gold that other explorers sought, but had waters teeming with so many cod that Cabot claimed he had difficulty sailing. Cabot's "discovery" of the Grand Banks, with its riches of codfish, stimulated English colonization of North America, the same way gold rushes of the middle and late 1800s lured settlers to the West Coast and Alaska.

Thirty-seven years after Cabot reached Newfoundland, when Jacques Cartier "discovered" the St. Lawrence River and claimed Canada for France, he noted that there were 1,000 Basque fishing vessels in the area. The Basques had been fishing off the coast for hundreds of years, but they didn't claim the land, in order to keep their discovery secret.

In the years before refrigeration, salt cod made European voyages of discovery possible all over the world, and New England cod was sent to markets throughout Europe. In 1640, the Massachusetts Bay Colony shipped out 300,000 cod. Millions of dollars were made on the cod fisheries, giving rise to the "codfish aristocracy" of New England.

By the twentieth century, the development of machine-powered ships, ground-scouring draggers, and the use of sonar to locate schools of fish led to overfishing and the collapse of the local cod fishery.

Aug. 1

Lammas Day, or "Loaf Mass Day," when the ancients celebrated the wheat harvest and the first loaves of bread were baked. Many green spaces in England were called Lammas lands. These lands were common lands for nine months of the year but were reserved for the sole use of their owners for the three months when the wheat was growing. On Lammas Day, the lands were reopened to the public.

Aug. 2

Black wild cherries ripen on the border of a field in Farmington, Connecticut. Their fruit consists of a pulpy covering and an indigestible seed. Robins ingest the berries, extract nourishment from the pulp, and expel the seeds in a fertilizing pellet of waste.

Aug. 3

An oak tree photosynthesizes energy from the sun beside a canal near an abandoned mill in Lowell, Massachusetts. Some scientists estimate that as much as 40 percent of the tree's energy is shared with the creatures in the earth around it, a biologically teeming zone known as the rhizosphere, where a thimble of dirt may contain a million bacteria and several miles of fungal hyphae.

Aug. 4

A mewing sound rises from a honeysuckle bush in the backyard, but it's not a cat, it's a gray catbird the size of a robin. Catbirds respond to imitation calls. Try it.

Aug. 5

Humidity bother you? Lakes and oceans aren't our only source of moisture. The plants in five acres of forest expire a swimming pool–ful of water into the air each day.

Aug. 6

A bumblebee browses among the flowers in the front yard. Its homing instinct is incredible.

Researchers have found that a bee can find its way back to its hive from a distance of two miles with its eyes covered.

Aug. 7

At dusk, brown bats venture out in search of insects. Some people may fear bats, but they're the only mammals capable of self-powered flight. These voracious insect-eaters catch as many as 600 mosquitoes an hour and will eat their body weight each night. We would have to eat about 80 pizzas to come close. Bats stay in their caves on rainy nights, alerted to inclement weather by the change in air pressure, which they probably detect in their inner ears.

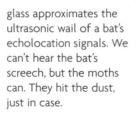

Aug. 8

A cloud of moths flutters around a lantern at a cocktail party in Beverly, Massachusetts. One wag rubs his fingers around the rim of a wine glass and makes it sing. The moths drop to the ground. It's not magic. The song of the wine glass approximates the ultrasonic wail of a bat's echolocation signals. We can't hear the bat's screech, but the moths can. They hit the dust, just in case.

Aug. 9

Captured in a headlight on Route 95, an opossum with big black eyes, a pointed nose, whiskers, and a long ratlike tail freezes and plays dead. It's a bad decision, because a speeding truck rumbles over it. The opossum has a very small brain; some experts think that it overloads in the face of danger, resulting in a comalike trance.

Aug. 10

Out on the Allagash River, an undulating string of ducklings follow in their mother's wake. They can't fly until they are three months old. In the meantime, many fall prey to snapping turtles, hawks, and motorboats. Ducks paddle at a top speed of 1.4 feet per second. When threatened, though, they can pump their webbed feet like pistons and hydroplane across the water at 6.6 feet per second. That's faster than most people can swim.

Aug. 11

A yellowjacket descends on a fly, stings it to death, and makes a beeline to its nest with the cumbersome bundle. By the end of the summer, only the pregnant female yellowjackets remain alive. They'll hibernate in wood piles and hollow stumps until next spring.

Aug. 12

An antlion, or "doodlebug"—brown and half an inch long, much of it pincers—sits at the bottom of a sandy hole in Bennington, Vermont, waiting for an ant to fall in. When it does, the "lion" seizes it and sucks out its vital juices. The doodlebug is the larval phase of a transparent-winged, dragonfly-like insect that will eventually patrol the edge of woodlands.

Aug. 13

A green tomato hornworm four inches long ravages a tomato leaf, and the plant goes into its "Star Wars" defense. The leaf's unwounded neighbors activate proteins designed to give the caterpillars a dose of indigestion. A recent study found that the wounded leaf emits an electrical signal that warns of the attack. The hornworm, named for the spinelike horn on its last body segment, is the larval stage of a moth. Soon it will become a dusky gray sphinx moth, with a five- or six-inch wingspan.

Aug. 14

A young beachgoer overturns a rock in the gravelly shallows of Echo Lake in Franconia, New Hampshire, and sends a four-inch-long crayfish scurrying for cover. These lobsterlike scavengers are nocturnal. They feed mostly on small plants and fish that they shred with their claws. They will pinch your finger if you let them.

Aug. 15

If birds fly close to the ground, you can expect rain. Birds fly in the path of least resistance, and it's easier to fly close to the ground when a low-pressure system is passing through.

Grasshopper

Aug. 16

A milk snake slithers under the garage. Handsome, harmless reptiles two feet long, gray with black and brown rings, milk snakes are nocturnal and are rarely seen. They live near barns and pick off mice. Rubes thought they milked cows when nobody was looking.

Aug. 17

Under the moonlight, an orange-brown *Polyphemus* moth rests on a rotten stump in Cranston, Rhode Island. The eyespots on its unfurled wings fool predators into thinking they're seeing an owl.

Aug. 18

A cinnamon brown Carolina locust, or grasshopper, pops up in front of a lawnmower in Lawrence and takes wing. Worldwide, grasshoppers consume more grass than all grazing animals combined.

Aug. 19

A trout leaps out of the water of Sebago Lake. Some say the fish rise when spooked by the shadow of a large bird; others say they rise to escape predatory fish or shake off parasites. Actually, the fish have acute eyesight and rise to catch insects flying just above the water.

Aug. 20

Fall webworms congregate in their unsightly silken webs on roadside trees. Unlike the tent caterpillar, webworms enclose leaves and small branches in their nests. The fuzzy tan caterpillars eventually morph into tiger moths.

Aug. 21

A Boston resident draws a glass of tap water. The same water may have quenched the thirst of a dinosaur 65 million years ago. Water is recycled endlessly. Sea water evaporates, falls as rain, and returns to the ocean by river or stream. Some estimate that it takes

3,200 years to recycle the world's 326 million cubic miles of water. Twenty thousand cycles ago, the dinosaurs ruled.

Aug. 22

Canada goldenrod, with plumelike pyramids of tiny yellow flowers, begins to blossom in fields and overgrown pastures. There are more than a dozen types of goldenrod in New England, including the lance-leaved, with flowers at its branch ends, and the blue-stemmed, with scattered tufts of flowers.

Aug. 23

Sparrow-sized barn swallows—steel blue with a creamy belly and rusty throat—congregate on a telephone wire in Alton, New Hampshire, before migrating south to Argentina. Unlike most birds, barn swallows migrate by day, feeding on mosquitoes and other bugs along the way.

Aug. 24

On a south-siding hill in the Green Mountains, a black widow spider sits under a rock. It's recognizable by the distinctive scarlet hourglass on its belly. The black widow is the most poisonous spider in the world, but its bite is rarely fatal and it seldom attacks humans. Encounters were much more frequent in the early days, when these spiders wove webs across privy seats in outhouses.

Aug. 25

Just before the rain, you might hear the clucking of a "rain crow," a rapid *ka-ka-ka-ka* trailing off to a *kowp, kowp, kowp*. This is the call of the yellow-billed cuckoo, a shy bird that skulks in dense vegetation. Cuckoos are particularly fond of furry

Barn swallows

gypsy moth caterpillars, which most birds avoid. They may pluck clumps of hair off the bodies before they dine. When a cuckoo's stomach gets clogged with hairs, it might cough up its stomach lining, which is replaced by a new one. Farmers love cuckoos, not only for their diet, but because they have a habit of calling when a storm is approaching.

Yellow warbler

Aug. 26

In Rock Harbor on Cape Cod, a young beachcomber encounters a patch of black sand. The sand has been discolored by bacteria that live without oxygen in the muddy, organically rich sand.

Aug. 27

Terns—white, pigeon-sized "sea swallows" with black caps and forked tails—flock up on Monomoy Island off the "elbow" of Cape Cod as they get ready to head for their wintering grounds in South America.

Aug. 28

Yellow warblers with a light olive tinge to their backs leave their summering grounds near a tributary of the Shawsheen River and begin the long flight to their wintering ground in Mexico. This warbler is one of the principal victims of the cowbird, a much larger bird that lays its eggs in the nests of other birds. If the warbler finds out, it buries the interloper's egg and often several of its own as well.

Aug. 29

An iridescent red eft creeps across the damp forest floor like a salamander from Mars. Birds don't eat the otherworldly amphibian; its gaudy pigment warns them of its loathsome taste. The eft is a newt in its terrestrial phase. Soon it will lumber into a pond and stay there.

Aug. 30

A young angler digs for worms in an abandoned cornfield. He won't have to look far. Healthy soil contains as many as 2 million worms per acre. They expel 700 pounds of nutrient-rich castings per day.

Aug. 31

The leaves of some trees begin to turn color early. Salt-damaged trees along highways are the most noticeable, but a few trees in the forest will turn, too. Rural folk call them "Judas trees."

SEPTEMBER IS THE MONTH OF THE LONG GOOD-BYE. As the days grow short and the nights grow cold, we reluctantly say "so long" to summer. There's still plenty of warm weather left, but time is of the essence.

Most insects will die, depriving birds of a primary food source. Grapes and berries ripen and fall, just in time for the birds to gorge themselves before heading south for winter. Female yellowjackets buzz listlessly in sunny spots before seeking shelter underground. Crows and ravens come in from the hinterlands to assemble in winter rookeries.

Birds aren't the only animals that seek safety in numbers during cold weather. Ladybugs do, too. You might see the rotund orange-and-black beetles congregating in sunny spots, even on your windowsill.

During the summer months, ladybugs lead solitary lives as they prey on mealybugs and aphids. When the days grow short, they congregate. They'll spend the winter in masses of hundreds and thousands under pine needles and leaf litter, where they enter a hibernation-like state called *diapause*, in which their metabolic rate slows to as little as one-tenth of average. They remain inactive all winter and will reanimate in the spring.

The ladybug is one of the few insects that people find endearing. Its name often has religious significance: ladybug is short for "Our Lady's Bug." In German, the insect is known as *marienkafer*, or "Mary's beetle." In French, it's *bête à bon dieu*, the "creature of God." The Dutch call it *lie veheerbeestje*, or "dear Lord's little creature." In Hebrew, it's *parat Moshe Rabbenu*, or "creature of Rabbi Moses." In Greek, ladybugs are *paschalitsa*, or "little ones of Easter."

The eerie nocturne of the cricket is the song of September. From sub-urban subdivisions to rural pasture, its ceaseless drone enlivens the night. Only the male cricket chirps, a sound it makes by rubbing its two front wings together. You're most likely to hear a field cricket, but you may be lucky and encounter a North American snowy tree cricket. The tree cricket is also known as the "thermometer cricket" because you can determine the temperature by counting the chirps it sounds in 15 seconds and adding 40.

For most animals making a lot of noise in the early autumn, sex is a motivating factor. The crickets' chirp serves as a courting song to attract females and as a fighting song to repel other males. The Chinese used to collect crickets and have singing contests.

Early in the month, the cricket chorus creates a lively droning in the backyard; later, when the cold brings them inside, a cricket chirping in the cellar is one of the first signs of fall. The presence of a "hearth cricket" is said to be good luck.

As the days grow short, the production of chlorophyll, the green pigment, ceases in plants, allowing other colors to blaze briefly before trees and bushes shed their leaves in anticipation of the long winter drought.

Acorns ripen and fall, littering the backyard and keeping squirrels and chipmunks busy. These irascible rodents "squirrel away" the harvest. Chipmunks are "dormant" sleepers. They hoard the nuts in burrows. Squirrels remain active during winter warm spells. They often bury nuts underground. In midwinter, you may see them digging in the snow, trying to uncover them.

Ducks move south in small numbers from their summering grounds on lakes and ponds to saltwater bays and harbors, where the water rarely freezes. Loons also leave the lakes and ponds. They spend the winter in splendid isolation in deeper water off the coast.

As the sun rises, a broad-winged hawk glides in an effortless circle on outstretched wings a mile above Wachusett Mountain. As the ragged-winged raptor scans the ledges for mice, squirrels, and other targets of opportunity, it is joined by dozens of others. It's the peak of the hawk migration. As many as 20,000 birds have been seen above the mountain in a day. Like gliders, the birds rise on thermals and gain enough altitude to soar for several miles, thus saving precious energy for their flight to South America. If you see more than five birds riding a thermal, it's called a kettle. Some kettles hold several thousands.

An early snowy owl appears on Belle Isle Marsh in East Boston as they return south. These voracious predators find our winter weather relatively balmy after spending the summer in the Arctic. Large white birds with a round head and a five-foot wingspan, they are creatures of the open country, and are rarely seen on trees. You might spot them on the ground, a rooftop, or a fencepost.

Red foxes take advantage of the extra darkness to extend their nightly rounds into the suburbs of Burlington, Vermont. You might not see them, but they're out there. They have adapted well to urban environments and can be found in most cities and towns.

Foxes are primarily nocturnal in urban and suburban areas, mostly as an accommodation to humans. Unlike their more noisy cousins, the coyotes, foxes prefer to hunt by stealth, like cats, rather than by pursuit, leading some to call them the "catlike canine."

Foxes are not large, though their relatively long legs and bushy tails can be deceiving. They generally weigh 7 to 15 pounds and reach about 3 feet in length, though their tails may add another foot and a half. It's not unheard of to see them during the day. When they are spotted, particu-larly if they feel secure in the neighborhood, they have the disarming habit of holding their ground and staring at intruders. But they are generally harmless to people—they would rather run than fight.

Foxes are better hunters than raccoons and subsist mainly on squirrels, though they are not above sampling garbage from an open container or helping themselves to pet food left outdoors.

As the cidery smell of dead leaves and rotting apples fills the air, field mice abandon the backyard and skitter into the cellar, where they will winter over in relative comfort. While pumpkins turn orange on the vines and sunflowers hang heavy in the faltering sunlight in Union, Maine, robins fatten up on earthworms in preparation for their long flight to Alabama, though some winter over.

A solitary woodchuck waddles into the riverside burrow where it will sleep through the worst of the ice and snow. Flocks of Canada geese migrate south under cover of darkness.

But everything is relative. After tourists hightail it south, grosbeaks, nuthatches, and other visitors from the great white frozen North move into our area, where they find the winter relatively warm.

As photosynthesis ceases, the leaves of a maple tree rustle in a light breeze. A maple tree hides nearly half its biomass in a great tangle of roots, which are woven into an even bigger web of fungus. The relationship benefits both. Trees can manufacture carbon from sunlight, water, and air, but their roots can't extract enough vital nutrients like phosphorus and nitrogen from the soil. Fungi contain enzymes that free phosphorous and nitrogen from the earth, but they can't manufacture carbon. So they share: the fungi take carbon from the roots of the trees and give the tree nutrients in return.

The underground web of fungi can also channel nutrients from one species of tree to another. A study done by the British Columbia Ministry of Forests found that, under certain conditions, birch seedlings growing in the sunlight funneled carbon to fir trees withering in the shade. The exchange was made via the underground network of fungi.

At the edge of Touisset Marsh in Warren, Rhode Island, rise the sausagelike stalks of a cattail. Native Americans treated the plant as a supermarket. In early spring, the young shoots and stalks were peeled and eaten raw or boiled. In late spring, the green flowerheads were husked and boiled. In early summer, the pollen heads were picked and eaten raw, or dried into flour. The cattail root was eaten anytime from late summer through winter. Horn-shaped sprouts growing from the roots were eaten raw or boiled for a few minutes. The roots themselves, an excellent source of starch, were crushed and dissolved in cold water and made into a flour, after draining and drying. Native Americans used mashed cattail flowers as a salve for cuts and burns; they used the sticky juice they found between young leaves as a styptic (to stop bleeding) and to numb an aching tooth. Indian babies nestled in cattail-lined diapers in cattail-padded papooses.

Sept. 1

Ragweed is in blossom. You'll see the heavy yellow flowers in clearings along the road. Native Americans made a yellow dye from the plant. During the Revolution, when tea was scarce, colonists drank a concoction brewed from the plant and called it "Blue Mountain tea."

Sept. 2

A flat-clawed hermit crab scuttles across a clam flat in Chatham, Massachusetts. When threatened, it withdraws into the walnut-sized shell it borrowed to protect its unarmored abdomen. An anemone or sponge may hitchhike a ride on its shell. When the crab grows bigger and abandons its shell for a larger one, it sometimes brings the hitchhiker along because it offers added camouflage.

Sept. 3

Once again, the sound of the mockingbird fills the air as the bird runs through its repertoire of imitations—anything from a squeaking wheelbarrow to the melodious song of a thrush—while perched atop a telephone pole. The birds were silent in late August during molting.

Sept. 4

Fuzzy wooly bear caterpillars—rust-colored with black bands—cross sun-warmed roads. Backwoods prognosticators say the amount of black on its bristles forecasts the severity of the winter. Actually, the amount of black indicates how near the caterpillar is to full growth before seeking shelter for the winter. It will eventually morph into a moth.

Sept. 5

The distinctive fluffy, gray-tan seed heads of phragmites waver in the breeze on the shore of Great Bay in New Hampshire. This invasive plant grows up to 20 feet tall and is easily recognizable. Early settlers used the sturdy stalks for thatching.

Wooly bear caterpillars

Sept. 6

In 1881, September 6 became known as the famous "Yellow Day," when smoke wafting from forest fires in Michigan blocked out the sun in New England and gave the landscape a brassy glow.

Sept. 7

On a mild morning, hatchling snapping turtles waddle out of their nests to the safety of the waters of College Pond in Plymouth, Massachusetts, where they'll spend the winter in the mud. The temperature of the nest during incubation determines the sex of the hatchlings: two-thirds of the way through the 9- to 12-week incubation, if the temperature in the nest is 84 degrees or hotter, the eggs will produce females; temperatures of 80 degrees or cooler will produce males.

Sept. 8

It's mating season for moose. You can expect the stilt-legged herbivores to show up in unlikely locations as young bucks start looking for love in all the wrong places. In recent years they've shown up in a swimming pool in Nashua and in the Lowell business district.

Sept. 9

At dawn, dew-soaked handkerchiefs of pearl gray dot the lawn. It's the overnight work of orb weaver spiders. Each of these yellow-brown spiders is connected to a web by a long signal line. When the spider feels a fly caught in the web, it runs out for breakfast.

Sept. 10

For hibernation, some woodchucks maintain separate dens located in well-drained slopes. They don't store food in the den; they just sleep there. Essentially, woodchucks eat half the year and sleep half the year.

Sept. 11

An orange-brown meadow jumping mouse with a white belly settles into the burrow it has been accessorizing for winter. This female has fattened up on seeds and nuts to a hefty 4.5 ounces. Her bed is a perfect sphere of grass in a burrow a foot or two under the ground. She'll curl up for the winter and awaken in April.

Sept. 12

Nighthawks head south in flocks, sometimes with as many as 3,000 birds. The name of this blue jay–sized predator is misleading. You often see them flying in the sunlight, and they're not really a hawk, though they do "hawk," or catch insects on the wing.

Sept. 13

Immature warblers head south. They're usually olive drab and difficult to identify.

Sept. 14

When cattle egrets first came to New England from the South, they tended to show up in the fall and quickly fly back south; later, they came in the spring to nest and raise young. Originally from Africa, the birds first made their appearance in the deep South about 100 years ago. You may see one of these white egrets with a stout yellow bill near any dairy farm.

Cattle egrets look for beetles and grasshoppers flushed from cover by grazing cows. This heronlike bird has been known to sit on the back of a cow, where it may look for ticks and flies in the cow's hair.

Sept. 15

Bright yellow Jerusalem artichokes blossom near streams and ponds. The plant is not from Jerusalem and it's not an artichoke. Native

Jerusalem artichoke

Americans called this plant "sun root" and grew the perennial for its tubers in their gardens on Cape Cod. Explorer Samuel de Champlain, who thought the roots tasted like artichokes, brought the plant back to France. When the plant arrived in Italy about 1633, it was called *girasole*, which means "turning to the sun." Somehow that became corrupted to "Jerusalem."

Sept. 16

The osprey, or "fish hawk," that nested on a seaweed-draped rock promontory off Deer Isle in Maine begins its long migration to Argentina, stopping to catch fish on its way. Brown on top and white below, you might recognize it from a distance by the distinctive bend at the "wrist" of its wing. It will soar high above the water until a fish nears the surface, then descend feetfirst to snatch and lift its silvery prey on feet equipped with sharp spiny projections to aid its grip.

Sept. 17

House mice seek shelter from storms ahead in cellars and behind walls. They followed the first Europeans to the New World and have established themselves all over the North American continent. Their relationship with man is called *commensal*, which means "sharing the table."

Sept. 18

Transparent, three-inch-long "glass eels," born in the Sargasso Sea off Bermuda, are coming in from the ocean and moving up creeks and estuaries. The immature eels will settle in bays, where they will acquire pigment and become known as "elvers." Some will remain in the estuary as adults, but others will migrate upstream, where they will remain for about five years before returning to the Sargasso Sea to breed.

Sept. 19

A female praying mantis with a spindly green body and a triangular head

Osprey

stands athwart a blade of grass in White River Junction, Vermont. She bobs her neck as she searches for prey with her incomparable compound eyes, but she spots a male praying mantis instead. The couple mate, a magic moment; then the female eats the lovestruck male.

Sept. 20

In iffy weather, a back-woodsman consults a pinecone, a prognosticator as accurate as any TV meteorologist. In dry weather the cone's scales shrivel, open up, and stand out stiffly. When rain is on the way, the scales absorb moisture in the air and tighten up.

Sept. 21

The Great Hurricane of 1938 mauled New England with wind gusts of up to 100 miles per hour. Rivers rose and flooded. There were 13½ feet of water in downtown Providence. Six hundred people died, and 275 million trees were snapped or uprooted in the Connecticut River Valley and the Green Mountains. Tiny local telephone companies went bankrupt, allowing the Bell system to gobble up what was left.

Sept. 22

A luckless picnicker steps into a poison ivy patch at the edge of the lawn and acquires an itchy rash. More than 50 million people will be affected by poison ivy this year. Dogs are not bothered by it but can spread it to unsuspecting humans who pat them. Cows can even eat poison ivy. It doesn't bother birds, either; fall migrants will feast on its berries.

Sept. 23

A mustard white butterfly dabbles at the ragweed patch at the edge of the forest. Some think this pale butterfly is a moth, but it's not. A moth's antennae are featherlike or wiry, and lack the clubbed tip common to the mustard white and other butterflies. Though most moths fly at night, some species are active during the day; butterflies are active only during the day.

Sept. 24

As their population soars, black bears begin turning up in bedroom communities, where they will raid birdfeeders and garbage cans and hibernate in culverts. Each bear requires a range of about 15 square miles. A bear has very poor eyesight and locates food—primarily plants, but also some insects, eggs, and small rodents—with its keen sense of smell.

Black bear

Sept. 25

In northern New England, the first frost appears on pumpkins about now.

Sept. 26

Puffball mushrooms spring up on lawns and pastures. The skull-shaped puffball looks like a bulky muffin with a rounded, baked-bun top. The cup-shaped puffball looks like a round tan stone. Mushroom collectors love to cook them. What do they taste like? Nothing. They acquire the taste of whatever they're cooked with.

Sept. 27

A red-eyed loon scampers across Squam Lake in New Hampshire as it strains to get up enough speed to fly. Its eyes are red because of a pigment in the retina that filters light when the bird is diving for fish underwater.

Sept. 28

Blackpoll warblers—common birds with black caps and bodies mottled with black, white, and gray— begin their marathon, an 86-hour, nonstop flight from the North Shore of Massachusetts to South America. In human terms, that's the equivalent of running nonstop four-minute miles for three and a half days. And these small birds fly their marathon over water.

Monarch butterflies

Sept. 29

Michaelmas Day. If your goose is cooked, you've got it made. In merry England, Michaelmas Day was one of the days of the year when quarterly rent bills came due. Tradition tells us: "If you eat a goose on Michaelmas Day, you will never want for money all year round." The superstition dates back hundreds of years, to a time when people often included a goose in their rent payments.

Sept. 30

It's the height of the monarch butterfly migration. What the orange and black butterflies lack in size, they make up in determination. More than 100 million of these magnificent migrators will brave headwinds, predators, and the Southeast Expressway to make the 3,000-mile trip to a stand of oyamel fir trees in Sierra Chincua, Mexico.

OCTOBER IS THE MONTH OF DEATH AND DECAY, when leaves crunch underfoot and the wind rattles through leafless trees. As the nights grow longer and the days grow cold, starlings flock up at dusk and wheel through the darkening sky before seeking safety in numbers under arches and bridges. The crickets that enlivened the night have grown silent. The frogs that harumphed in the wetlands have sought safety underground, as have the chipmunks and mice that skittered across the yard.

Most insects are dead or dying. Squirrels gather acorns recklessly and bury them in storage for the winter famine. Groundhogs, bears, and other hibernators seek shelter in dens below the frost line, where they'll sleep in relative comfort below the ice and sleet.

Brown bats hang from delicate feet in the musty corners of caves and barns. These tiny mammals can't fatten up for the winter on their high-protein, all-insect diet, so they sink into a torpor when the temperature drops beneath 40 degrees.

Millions of birds retreat south. Billions of leaves rot on the forest floor. Sparrows swoop and flutter over fields and grasslands and congregate on telephone wires in preparation for the long, dangerous trip south.

Some birds are world-class travelers. A banded 3.5-ounce yellowlegs once made it from Boston to Martinique, a distance of nearly 2,000 miles, in seven days. A blue-winged teal made the trip from the St. Lawrence River near Quebec to Guyana, 3,300 miles, in 27 days.

We rarely see migrating birds because most of them fly under cover of darkness, navigating by the stars or magnetic fields—nobody knows for sure. Researchers track the birds' movement with high-powered listening devices. Birders track their movement by focusing binoculars on the moon and waiting for a flock to pass. You may hear the honk of Canada geese, the quack of a duck, or some other birdly chitter-chatter if you're outside on a quiet night.

The full moon looms large on the horizon when the air is crisp as cider. The Abenaki Indians, or " People of the Dawn," called it the Red Leaf Moon. The early settlers had other priorities. They called it the Hunter's Moon.

On the last Sunday of the month, Daylight Saving Time ends. The sun seems to set an hour earlier, heightening the sense of darkness and foreboding. Trees, our largest and most long-lived plants, shut down food production in preparation for the winter drought. But the hardwoods don't quietly skulk into dormancy like skunks and groundhogs; they flare in a brilliant flash of color praised by poets and bus tour guides. New England's fall foliage display is particularly bright, primarily due to the millions of sugar maples that paint the hills orange, yellow, and red.

Cool October nights stimulate cells at the base of each leaf to choke off the supply of water in preparation for winter, when the ground is frozen and water is difficult to absorb. This shuts down the production of chlorophyll, the green pigment in the leaves, and allows xanthophyll, carotene, and anthocyanin pigments to predominate for a few days before the leaves dry out and fall to the ground. Anthocyanin is the pigment that makes morning glories blue. Carotene makes carrots orange and xanthophyll makes egg yolks yellow. Since production of these pigments depends on light, the leaves of a sugar maple might turn yellow in the shade and red in the sun. If early October is cloudy, leaves go from green to yellow. Sunny days and cool, clear nights generate reds, oranges, and purples and paint the hills with color. The yeasty aroma of decaying leaves and stagnant water underscores the eeriness of the quaking bog at Ponkapoag in Canton, Massachusetts. Shadows dance between shaggy-barked cedar trees and a few hearty crickets sing so long to summer as a solitary visitor clomps down the half-mile boardwalk erected by Professor William Babcock and his students at Eastern Nazarene College in 1947. After tunneling through a fragrant, shoulder-high stand of cedar, the boardwalk opens out into the bog. The bog's soupy surface is flecked with wild cranberries and framed by the silver stump of a water-logged white pine and the red flare of a swamp maple.

The bog was dug by a glacier during the last Ice Age. Enclosed by steep sides and poor drainage, the bog's acid-rich soil nourishes a peat deposit that breeds pitcher-plants, bladderworts, and other carnivorous plants. From the end of the boardwalk, you can hear cars whiz by on Route 128 and spot the red-and-white antenna on the summit of Great Blue Hill. Yet it isn't difficult to imagine that the glacier just retreated from this desolate spot. In fact, it did—12,000 years is a blink of the eye in geologic terms.

But the main attraction of the quaking bog is its floor—a dense, floating mat of sphagnum moss that isn't land or water, but something in between. Taking a step onto its shaking surface is a risky, sneaker-soaking proposition, like walking on a wave covered with a wet blanket.

Surrounded by such mystery, it's not hard to see why the early European expatriates who settled here feared the endless forest and sought guidance from the stars. The Pleiades, or "seven sisters," a star cluster 400 light years away, rises at dusk in the middle of the month and reaches its highest point around midnight on October 31. This is when the Celtic settlers observed Samhain, the midpoint between the first day of autumn and the first day of winter. On Samhain, it was believed that the line between the natural and supernatural blurred, granting free passage to evil beings from the land of the dead. To make their homes less desirable to unwanted guests, the settlers doused the fires in their hearths and cowered in darkness. Samhain was sometimes called the Witch's Sabbath. We now call it Halloween.

Oct. 1

There's still an apple or two yet to be plucked in the orchard. Tradition tells us if an apple's skin is rough, we're in for a rough winter.

Oct. 2

Sluggish from the cold, a two-year-old barn spider still maintains a web under a porch light, where the occasional moth, the spider's favorite meal, still flutters. Because of the short growing season in northern New England, it takes a barn spider two years to complete its life cycle. After its eggs hatch in late summer, the young spiders disperse and hibernate. The following spring, they spin their webs in shady locations and molt five to eight times, growing larger each time, like lobsters.

Oct. 3

In damp woods on the Green Mountains, you can still find witch-hazel in flower, the last of the trees to do so. Witch-hazels have yellow, whiskery flowers that turn into contorted, nut-shaped seedpods. The pods dry, shrink, and eventually explode with an audible pop, scattering seeds up to 30 feet from the parent. An astringent made from its tannin-rich bark and twigs is used on insect bites, sunburn, and as a soothing after-shave lotion. The early settlers believed the plant had magical powers and chose its branches when dowsing for water.

Oct. 4

Flocks of Canada geese honk and clatter as they navigate by night toward their wintering quarters on Chesapeake Bay. You're most likely to hear them at dawn or dusk. Conventional wisdom tells us that wizened old ganders lead the flock, but there's nothing conventional about wisdom, and ganders don't get wizened by wearing themselves out. That leaves the younger, heartier honkers to lead the pack. Some geese will remain in New England

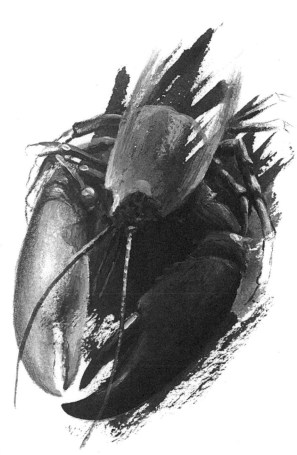

Oct. 7

Ravens—black birds similar to crows, but larger—begin to roost in the North Country. Exuberant birds that soar and tumble through the sky, ravens avoid civilization and are common only in the deep woods.

Oct. 8

Beavers, normally nocturnal, may become active during the day as they rush to store fresh branches under water to eat in winter, when ice will cover their ponds.

Oct. 9

Four inches of snow fell on Boston on this date in 1703.

for the winter, especially if there are golf courses or open reservoirs nearby.

Oct. 5

A lobsterman removes a 1¼-pound chicken lobster from a trap in Boston Harbor. To allow for growth, the crustacean must shed its shell. During the five years it took for the animal to reach legal size, it shed its shell about 25 times.

Oct. 6

Spotted salamanders lumber across the forest floor on bowed legs and burrow into the leaf litter for their long winter snooze.

Oct. 10

Humpback whales off Cape Cod fatten up on schools of sand eels before migrating to the Caribbean, where they will fast all winter, mate, and give birth.

Oct. 11

Out in the Blue Hills, a chubby rattlesnake suns itself on a warm rock near its ancestral den. The snake will bask in the sun all day and sleep all night before going into hibernation. Native Americans considered the appearance of the reptile to be an omen. They avoided killing them and hotly debated the significance of each encounter.

Oct. 12

Five hundred years ago, Columbus "found" a continent that didn't know it was lost. In unknowing tribute, a finicky gardener plucks a plantain from his meticulously maintained lawn. One of our most common weeds, this invasive European import followed so quickly on the invaders' heels that Native Americans called it the "white man's footprint."

Oct. 13

Up in the North Country, a snowshoe hare with ears as big as a donkey's sheds its dusky coat for winter white. If there's not much snow, the hapless hare will stick out like a bunny in a wolf pack and become easy prey for a bobcat or coyote.

Oct. 14

Fall foliage peaks about now.

Oct. 15

Pick those tomatoes. It's about time for the first killing frost.

Oct. 16

Keep an eye out for rain. Folk wisdom says that if there's much rain in October, there will be much wind in December.

Oct. 17

At dusk, starlings gather by the thousands to roost under bridges. The birds are descended from 100 starlings released in Central Park in New York in 1890 by Eugene Schieffelin, who wanted to introduce all the birds mentioned in Shakespeare

Rattlesnake

into the New World. There are now hundreds of millions of starlings in the United States.

Oct. 18

Snapping turtle hatchlings burrow into the mud at the bottom of a pond, where they will winter over in the muck. Some hatchlings winter over in their nests. Without a snowy winter to insulate them, the young turtles will die.

Oct. 19

A fisher cat, the secretive "black cat" of Colonial times, stalks a squirrel in a treetop in the Berkshires.

Once nearly extirpated in the area, the fisher is making a comeback and moving into suburbia. Though they're rarely seen, there are as many of these large weasels in the state now as there were in Colonial times, according to some experts.

Oct. 20

A scimitar-winged herring gull wheels out over the harbor. Civilization has answered this prodigious scavenger's dream by providing plenty of garbage to munch on. But landfills are closing and the birds' numbers are dwindling.

Turkey vulture

Oct. 21

A flock of ragged-winged turkey vultures circles over Mount Tom, waiting for something to die. These crow-sized scavengers have weak feet and talons. They rely on road kill and other carrion for food, though they have been known to chow down on grasshoppers and pumpkins in a pinch. Turkey vultures are recent arrivals to the Northeast, moving north as the climate warms.

Oct. 22

It's an active month for sparrows. They're seed-eaters, and the fields are

Snapping turtle hatchlings

Cormorant

full of them. Sparrows eat bushels of weed seeds that might otherwise compete with next year's crops.

Oct. 23

With a squawk and a flutter, a squadron of black ducks descends on Dorchester Bay. They'll winter over on the bay before returning to inland ponds to mate.

Oct. 24

A black cormorant stands on a buoy in Boston Harbor and spreads its wings to dry. Medieval fishermen considered the needle-beaked fish-eaters evil because the birds competed with them for food. The bird's oblique-angled wings became the inspiration for gargoyles.

Oct. 25

A coyote with a dead squirrel in its mouth trots into its den on Duxbury Beach, just south of Boston, where there's plenty of prey. When the European colonists first arrived, the white pine forest extended from Maine to the Great Lakes. Glib pioneers told tin-horns that a squirrel could travel from Maine to the Mississippi without leaving the branches of white pine. The first sawmill in the New World was erected in York, Maine, in 1623. Now squirrels would be better off taking the bus.

Oct. 26

Time for the fall turnover in College Pond in Plymouth, Massachusetts. The water of the lake is divided into distinct temperature zones. Like vinegar and oil, the layers float on top of each other. In the summer, the warm temperature heats the top, or epilimnion layer; a diver will feel the cold of the middle, or metalimnion layer, when he enters it at about 10 feet below the surface. As the water at the surface gets colder and heavier, it sinks and mixes with the deeper water, mixing nutrients and water life in the process.

Oct. 27

A flash of purple on a south-facing hillside. It's a New England aster, one of the last blooming flowers. It got its name from the Greek word for "star."

Oct. 28

The broken bodies of night-flying crossbills and siskins litter the pavement in Boston's financial district. The birds met their demise at the business end of a mirror-walled skyscraper. Their migration routes predate downtown Boston by thousands of years.

Oct. 29

Get your rakes ready. One good-sized maple tree can produce enough dead leaves to carpet half an acre.

Oct. 30

Be on the lookout for Indian Summer, the fat season after the crops are in, before the cold arrives in earnest. The technical definition of Indian Summer is a period after the killing frost of at least three days when the temperature does not drop below 40 degrees. These are the smoky days when the sun rises red and the moon is orange and even the animals don't move.

Indian Summer provided a brief period of leisure for the Native Americans.

Oct. 31

A cat's eyes glow as it races in front of a car's headlights in Brattleboro, Vermont. The back of a cat's eyes have a mirror-like structure that reflects light, allowing it to see better in the dark. It also produces eyeshine. Early man thought cats' eyes opened a porthole into the fires of hell and gave them a wide berth. Trick or treat.

NOVEMBER IS A MONTH OF ANTICIPATION. THE TREES are bare and the woods are quiet except for the crunch of squirrels skittering through dead leaves, looking for acorns to munch on in the cold months ahead. Most birds have headed south, except the blue jays that screech a warning of your presence and the exuberant chickadees that serenade you with their *rat-a-tat* calls. A groundhog has crawled into its den beside the Blackstone River, where it will avoid the bitter chill of winter below the frost line. Even the earthworms have burrowed down to where the soil is warm.

A few yellowjackets still fly lethargically in the warm air over sunny decks and driveways, forestalling their inevitable death when the ground freezes hard. The frogs that made such a racket in the springtime are now safely ensconced in the mud. Turtles, too. Even the beavers have retreated into their dens before ponds freeze over. A black bear drowses near hibernation in its winter den in a culvert below the highway.

The chipmunks that danced around the woodpile are nodding in their burrows, which they have insulated with leaves. The garter snake that slithered near the garage has denned with other garters, sometimes dozens.

It is a gray month, the cloudiest; the sun is blotted out by the rain, snow, or clouds at least 50 percent of the time. It's one of the wettest months, too, with more than 4.2 inches of rain or snow, mostly rain.

Under the Beaver Moon, in a clearing in the woods, a sapling rises from the stump of a dead chestnut tree. These magnificent trees once shaded main streets and were the pride of many small towns, until 1904, when Asian chestnut trees were imported to the New York Zoological Park. The Asian trees carried a fungus blight that soon spread across the country. By 1950, nearly every chestnut tree in the country was dead or dying. Chestnut saplings still grow near the stumps of the dead trees in the forest. The saplings grow to be about 12 feet tall, then the bark begins to furrow, a patch of orange blisters appears on the bark, fruiting bodies of the fungus appear, and then these chestnuts die, too.

As the weather grows colder, deer seek out south-facing hillsides and congregate in evergreen forests, where there's safety in numbers and protection from the snow. The old and weak will perish. Bobcats, foxes, and fishers routinely visit the carcasses as if they were suet bags.

Deer are not creatures of the deep forest, which lacks underbrush and low, succulent vegetation; they live on the edge of society, where they nibble on the buds of the young plants that occupy the border between forest and field. They're also fond of acorns and apples. As their forest-edge habitat becomes squeezed by suburbanization, they frequently munch on ornamental bushes around homes.

Deer are the biggest wild animals most of us will encounter, and we're more apt to see them than ever. Wildlife officials estimate that the New England deer population has doubled in the last ten years as the forest is cleared. Home ranges are thought to be shared by related females (does), who form matriarchies and exclude related males when they reach maturity.

Deer are silent animals that appear like ghosts and disappear just as quietly. You're most likely to see them at dawn and dusk on the borders of forests and fields. If you've seen them once, you're apt to see them again. They generally have small ranges and stay within a square mile for long periods of time. And they're creatures of habit. They usually bed down in the same location every night, browse at the same three or four feeding areas, and drink from the same water source each day.

A turkey lumbers into the clearing in Easton, Massachusetts. Wild turkeys are deep-woods birds that were extirpated in New England as the forest was cut down. The last of Massachusetts' native birds was shot and killed in 1851 on Mount Tom, which may have been named after the male turkey. Attempts to reintroduce gobblers in the state between 1900 and 1960 failed because wildlife officials were using farm-raised turkeys. In 1971, biologists began trapping wild birds in upstate New York and releasing them in the Berkshires. There are now about 15,000 turkeys in the Bay State. Similar programs have been successful in other New England states.

Wild turkeys live as far east as Andover, Plymouth, and Cape Cod. But you rarely see them. They are smart and elusive birds that travel in flocks and avoid civilization, even though they are now living in suburbs of Boston. With their small heads, bulky bodies and skinny legs, they look awkward, but they can sustain flight at 30 to 35 miles per hour and reach a speed of 55 miles per hour for short periods. Turkeys can run 25 miles per hour, covering the ground in four-foot strides. And they have excellent eyesight; their wide-angle, color vision is said to be six times better than humans'.

Native Americans were fond of turkeys. Some tribes even domesticated them. Though the Pilgrims hunted turkeys, they also brought some with them from Europe. In the late 1400s, Spanish explorers took wild turkeys from the Southwest to Spain, where farmers bred the birds. By the mid-1500s, turkeys were being raised in Italy, France, and England. Benjamin Franklin proposed that they be named our national bird.

Few can mention turkeys without Thanksgiving. The Pilgrims at Plimoth Plantation did have a feast after their first harvest in the New World, most likely in early October of 1621, but it wasn't an annual event. We owe the holiday to indomitable New Hampshire–born editor Sarah Josepha Hale, the composer of "Mary's Little Lamb," who lobbied hard for a Thanksgiving holiday. President Abraham Lincoln first decreed that the holiday be held on the last Thursday in November. In 1939, Franklin Delano Roosevelt changed the date to the fourth Thursday in November to ensure a lengthy Christmas shopping season in the event that there were five Thursdays in the month of November.

Nov. 1

With a rustle of wings, a flock of pigeons with iridescent purple heads flies out of the path of a pedestrian on Boston Common. The most urban of birds, pigeons scramble for scraps along the sidewalk and will eat almost anything. These prolific birds were introduced by the early settlers. They raise four or five broods annually and will breed during winter.

Nov. 2

Weasels quit the deep woods and hang out around the banks of streams, where there is more food. The slithery, 16-inch-long predators sometimes keep a cache of dead rodents under a log.

Nov. 3

Twittering flocks of snow buntings are down from Canada. These small, sparrow-sized birds, brown with white wings, seek out barren places and may be found on the dunes at Plum Island in Newburyport or on inland fields, seeking grass and weed seeds.

Nov. 4

Screech owls, about 10 inches tall with prominent ear tufts and large yellow eyes, have become accustomed to the suburbs of Worcester. You often hear their call, a tremulous descending whistle, soft purrs, or trills. At night during the breeding season (which begins in late winter), screech owls protect their territory aggressively and will dive-bomb intruders. When discovered during the day, the owls freeze and rely on their protective coloration.

Nov. 5

Canada geese from northern Canada pass over at about this time. You sometimes hear them honking just before dawn, when they're looking for a pond or river to rest during the daylight hours.

Screech owl

water harbors to breed. These remarkable panfish are born symmetrical, with eyes on both sides of their heads, and swim much like other fish. As they grow older, their eyes migrate to the right and their body flattens to take on the familiar appearance of the pancake-thin bottom-dweller with both eyes on top of its well-camouflaged body.

Nov. 8

Out behind the barn in Winooski, Vermont, a deer mouse scurries by with a mouthful of milkweed. The mouse will use the fluff to line the abandoned mockingbird nest it adopted for the winter.

Nov. 6

Flocks of snow geese rest on Lake Champlain on their long flight south from Greenland to the ocean off New Jersey and the Outer Banks of North Carolina. The only wild, white goose commonly found in the East, they're unmistakable big white birds with black primary feathers on their wings and a distinctive black "grin patch" on their pink bills. Snow geese are one of the first birds to migrate north in the spring. They will be on the move again when there's still snow on the ground.

Nov. 7

Winter flounder move into the shallows of salt-

Nov. 9

The weather is cooling, but the sun is still cranking away. It provides 290 watts of heat over each square yard of Earth, as much as a hair dryer on low heat, but our weather is cooling due to the tilt of the planet at this time of year.

Canvasback ducks

Nov. 10

Incoming canvasback ducks—tough birds with white bodies, black chests, and reddish heads with low foreheads—arrive from Manitoba to settle for the winter in the waters off Connecticut. The large, V-shaped flocks were once a familiar sight, but the ducks are good eating and their numbers have dwindled.

Nov. 11

Early settlers stacked evergreen branches against their houses to block the winds from cellars and floors and hold the snow when it arrived. Colonists called making the stacks "house banking."

Nov. 12

On their move south from their summering grounds on the Gaspé Peninsula, gannets—pure white seabirds with a 6-foot wingspan and black tips on the ends of their wings—soar over the waters off Cape Cod. Gannets are powerful divers, hurtling into the water from a height of 50 feet and folding back their wings at the last moment before plunging deep into the water, where they prey on sand lances and other fish. If a nor'easter is blowing, you may see thousands of gannets near shore at Halibut Point on Cape Ann or off Race Point on Cape Cod. They spend the winter in warmer southern waters.

Nov. 13

A great horned owl, two feet tall with prominent ear tufts, sets up house-keeping on the Fenway in Boston, where it will kill a rat or some other rodent every night.

Nov. 14

Oak trees finally change color and lose their leathery brown leaves at about this time.

Nov. 15

A late-afternoon snow-storm on this date in 1967 dumped a foot of snow inland. Little more than an inch fell in Boston.

Nov. 16

As the ocean cools, late-migrating Kemp's Ridley turtles are stunned by the cold water and wash up on the beaches of Cape Cod Bay. The color of wet cement, they have a prominent "beak," which they use to grab crabs, shellfish, and other hard-shelled prey. It's usually the youngsters that wash up. They're between 12 and 15 inches long and weigh 5 to 10 pounds. They breed only in Mexico.

Nov. 17

More than 1,000 gray seals cavort in the waters off South Beach, a barrier island off Chatham on Cape Cod. Gray seals have larger heads than harbor seals and bigger noses, too. They can weigh as much as 800 pounds. Average life expectancy is 30 years for a male and about 45 years for a female.

Nov. 18

Watch for dovekies—chunky black-and-white seabirds the size of a star-ling—in the waters off the coast. Dovekies summer in the Arctic and winter in the waters off New England, but are some-times blown inland during storms. The Inuit eat

Gray seals

these plump birds in great numbers. They are thought to be one of the most abundant birds on the planet.

Nov. 19

A doughty yellowlegs stops at the clam flats on Dorchester Bay on the midway point in its migration from Canada to North Carolina. A slender, gray-streaked wading bird named for its long yellow legs, it wades up to its belly to spear minnows with its needle-like beak. Sometimes, it even swims.

Nov. 20

Hearty partridgeberries are still fruiting on the forest floor. Partridgeberry is a low-lying, trailing plant with oval, heart-like leaves and a red berry with two black dots on it. The dots are the result of a strange "mating" practice in which two of the plant's flowers fuse and combine into the fruit. Animals and survivalists eat them, but they don't taste like much.

Nov. 21

Humpback whales head south to the Caribbean breeding grounds, where they sing their lovely courting songs. Older males, past breeding age, stay on for the winter. They don't sing anymore.

Nov. 22

Common eiders, in groups called rafts, bob on waves off Monomoy. As many as half a million eiders may congregate here, supported by millions of mussels. These large ducks with long, sloping bills eat mainly first- and second-year mussels; the shells of the older mussels are too thick. Before the invention of synthetics, the eider's down was prized for its loft and its insulating qualities. The fluffy down was once collected from their nests on islands off the coast of Maine. It's still collected in Iceland.

Nov. 23

Red-breasted mergansers start heading south. The male has a green head, gray sides, a white neck ring, and a rusty breast. The female is gray, with a brown head and a white breast. They prefer lakes, but when lakes freeze, they head for the sea. It's the only merganser regularly found on salt water. This merganser is a diving duck; it survives mainly on fish it captures after a swift underwater pursuit.

Nov. 24

On this date in 1881, Alexander Crowell shot and killed the last cougar in Vermont. The 182-pound, 7-foot-long cat shot near Barnard is now in the state collection in Montpelier.

Nov. 25

Pilot whales migrate along the coast off Cape Cod. They're about 20 feet long, all black with a white chest patch and a bulging forehead. Sometimes, if the wind is high and the water murky, they become confused and get stranded. Their distress cries bring other

Junco

whales to their aid, but they often become stranded, too.

Nov. 26

On this date in 1898, a northeast gale sank some 300 boats and ships, including the *Portland*, a passenger ship that went down off Cape Cod with about 160 aboard.

Nov. 27

Juncos come in from the northern forest to winter over in fields, gardens, and parks. This sparrow-sized gray bird is a frequent visitor to bird- feeders. Some people call them "snow birds."

Nov. 28

Male white-tailed deer are in rut now. They slash angrily at trees with their antlers, to mark their ter- ritory and to get in shape in case there is competi- tion for the local does. White-tailed deer got their name from the large white tail or "flag," which is all you see when the animal bounds away.

Nov. 29

Brant, geese that fly in clusters instead of the distinctive V formation, return to their winter quarters on Quincy Bay from their summering grounds in the Arctic. Similar to Canada geese, but smaller, brant feed on eelgrass. In the 1930s, a disease nearly wiped out the plant and the brant population declined. They're still making a slow recovery.

Nov. 30

Some lavender asters still blossom on south-facing spots. Tradition tells us that flowers that bloom in late autumn are a por- tent of a bad winter.

DECEMBER IS THE MONTH OF DARKNESS AND DESPAIR, when the ancients dreaded the inevitability of snow and the possibility of hunger. Rural folk call it the "locking time," a season of solitude when the ground is frozen hard and the forest is gray and cold. Most birds have migrated; many animals are in hibernation. The silence is deafening.

Anxiety reaches its peak on December 21, the Winter Solstice, our shortest day, with nearly 15 hours of darkness.

But the darkness has a silver lining. Our agrarian ancestors took heart in the fact that the days would now be lengthening. Though there was plenty of

winter ahead, there was now reason for optimism. The Winter Solstice became a celebration of rituals of death and rebirth.

In ancient Egypt, it was thought that the god-savior Osiris died on December 21 and was born again to a virgin at midnight. The ancient Romans had a riotous one-week festival known as Saturnalia, during which slaves supped with their masters and were allowed to do and say what they liked. In Scandinavia the festival was called *yule* (or *juul*). Great yule logs were burned to help the sun shine more brightly. Native Americans and neolithic hunters are believed to have celebrated the occasion as well. Cave paintings provide evidence, but the details are sketchy.

In the woodlands, the brilliant greens of summer finally surrender to the faded browns of mud and dormant plants. Trees stripped of their leaves creak and groan in the breeze as wind-whipped snow collects on ice-crusted beaver ponds. But there's still activity if you look hard enough.

A muskrat leaves its cattail-insulated lodge in Jaffrey, New Hampshire, to dig roots and tubers from the muck under the ice; unlike beavers, muskrats gather food all winter. A turtle, late for hibernation, swims under a thin skein of ice in Essex Junction, Vermont. Its body absorbs long wavelengths of light, raising its temperature above that of the water.

A pileated woodpecker sits out the winter in a hole in a dead maple in Kennebunk, Maine. The pileated doesn't migrate; its food source is right in the tree with it, carpenter ants and beetles.

A red squirrel chatters to warn a visitor away from its corner of a pine grove, where there are enough pinecones to keep him scrappy all winter. Tail down, nose to the ground, a scruffy coyote trots down a trail, its breath steaming as it follows the scent of a snowshoe hare.

Not every animal sinks into a winter torpor. Some diving beetles remain active during the winter, as do some adult newts and crayfish. You can sometimes see them under the ice. Of course, trout and other fish remain active under the water, as do the muskrats that feed on them. Beavers are still active under the ice, munching on branches they stored earlier during the fall.

Mussels and pill clams lie dormant in the mud, as do leeches and some turtles and frogs. Salamanders hibernate under logs near ponds and wet-lands. Cold-blooded toads and water snakes also winter under logs. The insect inhabitants of the water film—water striders, surface spiders, and springtails—hibernate under plant debris near the water.

But life is still fragile, particularly for the smaller animals, and no strate-gy will save them if the snow gets too deep over the ice and cuts off light and photosynthesis.

The stars seem particularly bright in the cold, clear winter skies. But there's less there than meets the eye. Though it appears that we can see a sea of stars, it's only an illusion. We tend to focus on what we see, not what we don't. Though the sky appears to be full of millions of stars, only about 3,000 are visible to the naked eye.

The planet Venus is visible at sunrise and sunset. Because of its appearance at dawn and dusk, the ancient Greeks thought Venus was two different planets and gave it two names: Phosphorus and Hesperus. Just before sunrise, you can spot Venus as the "morning star" on the southeastern horizon. It's one of the most easily recognized sights in the sky because of its brightness. Only the sun and the moon are brighter.

The red-tailed hawks that winter over in New England have adjusted their hunting techniques to the short days and cold nights. They are husky birds with four-foot wingspans and black-and-white striping on their chests. They have a bony ridge over their eyes that shades them in direct sunlight, much like a baseball cap, but makes them look angry.

In the warm weather, red-tails ride thermals and search for prey from thousands of feet in the air. In winter, they become perch hunters and much more accessible to earthbound viewers. You might see one of them on a telephone pole or a tree near a highway or river.

Opportunistic feeders, they pick off rabbits, mice, and other small rodents, a sick duck or gull, even an occasional cat. They are quite vocal and territorial. Their call is a hoarse cry or rasping scream. You often hear them call when they are harried by crows. Red-tails live 6 or 7 years, as much as 30 in captivity, and are reputed to be monogamous.

By the time ice began to form at the edge of New England ponds, Native Americans had left the coast and headed for the hills, where the landscape offers protection from wind and snow and the elevation creates fast-moving streams that don't freeze. By the mid-nineteenth century, ice had become a cash crop: fortunes were made by rural folk who harvested the ice on Otternick Pond in Hudson, New Hampshire, packed it in sawdust, and sold it to city folks in summer.

Now, science and central heating allow us to look on winter as inconvenient, not life-threatening, and refrigeration has allowed us all to have a little bit of winter in our kitchens all year long.

But that first sight of ice on a puddle still has the power to chill the heart. It takes about three weeks of subfreezing temperatures to freeze a pond solid enough to walk upon. That formula goes out the window when snow covers the pond, insulating it before it freezes completely.

When ice is so clear that you can see right though it, it was formed by water that froze slowly, eliminating air bubbles in the process. Ice clouded with impurities or mixed with snow is more difficult to see through and is often less safe to walk on.

Ice expands when it freezes; that's why it floats on water. As water freezes and unfreezes, expanding and contracting, it creates the potholes that plague our streets. When it gets very cold, ice contracts, creating the cracking and groaning noises on ponds in the dead of winter.

Fourteen thousand years ago, during the last Ice Age, snow and ice piled a mile deep over Boston. Responding to a buildup of carbon dioxide in the atmosphere, or a tilt in the Earth's axis, the glacier began to melt and slowly retreat to its present location in the Arctic. The sandy runoff from the melting ice created Cape Cod. Its scouring action scooped out the bow-shaped cirque at Tuckerman Ravine on Mount Washington. It left behind the distinctive kettle ponds of Cape Cod when chunks of ice became embedded in the earth and dropped rocks called glacial erratics like Agassiz Rock, a granite boulder the size of a cottage in Manchester-by-the-Sea. The whaleback, or esker, in Weymouth, Massachusetts, was created by streams of glacial runoff.

In this, the month of the Ice Moon, pre-Christian Germans found hope in the presence of evergreen trees, which they saw as a symbol of everlasting life. They lit fires before them as a symbol of hope.

By the eleventh century, the trees were decorated with bread and apples. The bread symbolized knowledge; the apples were inspired by the story of Adam and Eve and symbolized the fight of good against evil. They called them "paradise trees" and used them in religious plays. By the seventeenth century, many Germans decorated their homes with evergreens for Christmas. The tradition was brought to the United States by German settlers in the early 1800s.

Dec. 1

A flock of mewing gulls descends on a discarded bag on Penobscot Bay. You don't see many first-year herring gulls now. They have gone south and will be back in late spring. Older, crustier gulls tough it out.

Dec. 2

Christmas ferns still provide a splash of color in the forest. They got their name from the shape of their leaves, which end in a short spur like the toe of the Christmas stocking.

Dec. 3

The songbirds have gone south, so the caw of the crow is the song of dawn. These hearty New Englanders strut side streets and highways in search of roadkill and other targets of opportunity. Crows eat almost anything.

Dec. 4

Up in the North Country, a moose browses on the tips of a maple tree. This feeding machine will wander the woods all day, consuming as much as 50 to 60 pounds of twigs

Moose

each day. Moose are almost always on the move. That's why they rarely survive in captivity.

Dec. 5

The raccoon that tipped over the trash cans during the summer is sound asleep in a culvert. But the clever scavenger with the ringed tail and the bandit's mask is not a true hibernator; it will wake on warm winter nights and go looking for food.

Dec. 6

Spooked by a shadow, a fingerling fish darts off a ledge into the safety of deeper water off Gloucester. Alerted by the motion, a merganser dives and skewers the tiny fish. As the merganser breaks water and gulps for air, a gull descends and steals the silvery prize. Even in Gloucester Harbor, only the strong survive.

Dec. 7

How strong is that ice? Ice that is 1⅝ inches thick will hold a 170-pound

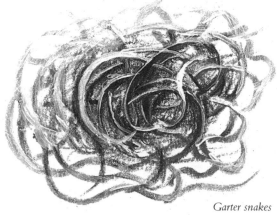

Garter snakes

man; 3 inches will hold a 570-pound snowmobile; and 6 inches of ice will hold a mid-sized car. But you never know where the weak spots are.

Dec. 8

A fist-sized bullfrog in hibernation rests partially buried in the muddy bottom of Jamaica Pond in Boston. The metabolism of the frog is very slow compared to warmer months, but it may swim around at times. Bullfrogs thrive in urban ponds, rich with fertilizer in which algae flourishes. Tadpoles eat the algae and live in the murky water, where they are largely unseen by birds.

Dec. 9

Trout, perch, and other freshwater fish remain active all winter, but if the snow cover gets too deep, underwater photosynthesis shuts shut down and the fish may die of oxygen deprivation.

Dec. 10

Out in the backyard, the garter snake is safely tucked in for the winter in an abandoned ant hill. Dozens of snakes sometimes den together. They feed mainly on earthworms and amphibians and secrete a foulsmelling liquid when alarmed.

Dec. 11

In 1963, a 23-day cold snap froze Dorchester Bay and Marblehead Harbor.

Dec. 12

The soft golds and browns of the Upper Cape are partly sand, partly the spartina grasses that anchor the sand. The grass spreads asexually by means of underground stems.

Dec. 13

Under cover of darkness, coyotes trot along the highway in search of a dead possum, squirrel, or other succulent roadkill. Coyotes have adapted to our presence. They sometimes den on median strips.

Dec. 14

Out in the deep woods, a snowshoe hare freezes at the crack of a twig. The rabbit's bulging eyes, set at the sides of its head, allow it to see 340 degrees (almost a full circle of its surroundings) without moving its head. Reassured, the hare hops back down the bunny trail.

Dec. 15

The eerie wail of a loon cuts through the predawn mist off Georges Bank. These deep-diving predators set up solitary stations on their wintering grounds off the coast. They sometimes follow fish to their deaths in dragger's nets.

Dec. 16

Harbor seals pull themselves out of the water to absorb the weak sunshine on a ledge off Lovell Island in Boston Harbor. These curious animals with the doglike faces are making a comeback locally now that sewage is being treated rather than discharged directly into the harbor.

Coyote

Dec. 17

A chattering flock of chickadees descends on a backyard birdfeeder. They're quickly joined by a nuthatch and a blue jay. Other birds often follow them to find a free lunch.

Dec. 18

With a throaty *grok*, a raven returns to its communal roost in the Berkshires. The ravens gather at night from 50 miles around. If one finds a tasty deer carcass, the rest of the flock will follow it to the feast in the morning.

Dec. 19

A ruffed grouse explodes from cover in a stand of pine trees. Locals call the grouse "partridges" and sometimes—because they make so much noise— "thunder chickens." Don't look for them in a pear tree. They hunker down in pine trees at this time of year.

Ruffed grouse

Dec. 20

Snow season is in full swing. But count your blessings—20 percent of the Earth's surface is permanently covered with snow. In some sections of Siberia, the permafrost extends to a depth of 5,000 feet.

Dec. 21

The Winter Solstice. Our shortest day. Only nine hours of daylight.

Dec. 22

Out in the backyard, deep in the cold mud below the frost line, a star-nosed mole goes about its business, tunneling after worms and slugs 20 inches below the surface. The 6-inch-long bundle of fur acquired its name from the fan of 22 pink tentacle-like projections radiating from its snout.

Dec. 23

A 30-pound bobcat hunkers down on its perch in an oak tree above a game trail in the high country. We rarely see them, but they're out there; the pancake-sized tracks in the snow and the bloody tufts of fur from its rabbit dinner give proof.

Dec. 24

Out in the Green Mountains, the most dangerous animal in America browses at the edge of a stand of pine trees. Each year, about 100 people are killed when cars collide with deer.

Dec. 25

The beginning of the French farmers' *jours des lots* ("days of fate"). Superstitious farmers set aside 12 onions, one for each month, and place a pinch of salt on each. On Epiphany, the onions are examined: If the salt has melted, the corresponding month will be wet; if the salt remains crystalline, the month will be dry. Closer to home, folk philosophers tell us that if Christmas is in snow, Easter is in mud.

Dec. 26

In 1778, the Hessian Storm hit southern New England. Temperatures dropped below zero, and 18 inches of snow fell. More than 50 people froze to death, including nine Hessian mercenaries who died at their posts in Newport. The American brig *General Arnold* foundered off Plymouth, going down with nearly 100 lost.

Dec. 27

A fertilized queen bee languishes in the attic. She will reproduce in the spring, when warm weather returns.

Dec. 28

Underneath the backyard, black ants have retreated into their deepest chambers, where they huddle together to fend off the chill. Little black ants, which live throughout the Unites States, are one of the least studied species.

Dec. 29

As the old saying goes: "If December is changeable and mild, the whole winter will remain a child."

Dec. 30

Out in the woods, a porcupine escapes the deepening snow by climbing a maple tree. The peaceful creature's hair has evolved into the barbed quills, or barbules, that have ravaged the faces of many a stray dog. It will survive on gnawed bark until the tree dies, then reluctantly waddle to another.

Dec. 31

Minks are still active near their dens along Nesenkeag Brook in Litchfield, New Hampshire, where Henry Thoreau once camped. The foot-and-a-half-long weasel with the lustrous fur feeds on small mammals, birds, fish, and frogs. They're nocturnal, but you might see a hole in the snow where one has pounced on a vole.

Bobcat

IN JANUARY, WINTER TIGHTENS ITS ICY GRIP AND THE
thin line between life and death becomes nearly
invisible to outdoor dwellers.

At the edge of a new housing development in
Marlborough, Massachusetts, a deer feeling the pressure of overpopulation takes a chance and browses
on tree buds at the border of the new clearing. The
hapless herbivore is spotted by a pet beagle, who
turns to investigate. The deer spooks and runs. The
dog instinctively gives chase. The howls of the beagle
are heard by a doberman and German shepherd, who
join the chase. The deer is quicker and more knowledgeable in the woods, but its stilt legs are unstable
on ice. When it steps out onto a frozen swamp, it
spread-eagles and its spindly front legs break. It is
unable to escape and is at the mercy of the dogs.
But domestic dogs don't kill to eat, they kill out of
instinct. The dogs only chew on the dying animal.

As day turns to dusk, the hounds return home to their bowls of kibble and the deer expires on the ice. But one animal's loss is another's gain. A coyote living near starvation locates the carcass by sense of smell and brings its pack over to feast on the dead deer.

At first light, a raven flies over and pecks at the carcass before returning to its rookery in the North Country; then it comes back with the flock in tow. Chickadees also feast on the suet until little is left. In the spring, birds use tufts of the animal's hair to line their nests, and bacteria specializing in decomposition consume any leftover meat. By the time a hiker walks by in May, all that's left is the sun-bleached skull.

Homes become an island of warmth in an inhospitable sea of snow and ice . . . and humans aren't the only ones seeking shelter.

If your attic isn't airtight, bats and squirrels may spend the winter up there. The bats hang by their feet from the rafters and hibernate, but the squirrels venture out during warm spells to look for food. You might hear them scrabbling around in the middle of the night.

Mice may find their way inside, too. But you rarely see them: they scavenge for food at night. Milk snakes might find their way into the cellar. They'll hibernate under debris and slither back outdoors in the springtime.

Ladybugs make their way in, too. You might see them snuggled in a corner of the ceiling. Skunks and even raccoons like to burrow under the house and spend the winter in relative warmth under a porch. Moths in their larval stages may winter over in a closet; spiders weave their webs in darkened corners. Fleas like it inside, too. They'll burrow into a comfy rug and may even breed there.

When the countryside is locked in snow and ice and food is hard to come by, hawks fly over the rivers of asphalt in search of unwary rodents that wander onto a dry patch on the side of the road. Crows congregate in trees on the lookout for dead possum, skunk, and other tasty morsels. Coyotes den in wooded median strips, where they too can take advantage of the free dinner provided by the automobile.

When winter winds rattle through the branches of leafless oak trees and slash across ice-coated ponds, a stand of pine trees in North Woodstock, New Hampshire, provides a welcome shelter. The trees' needles soak up snow melt and provide aromatic insulation for a wide range of wildlife. Chattering black-capped chickadees huddle in the branches. Gregarious, chipmunk-like red squirrels are found primarily in the white pine forest, where they feast all winter on pine cones. Spindle-legged white-tailed deer escape the snow in shadows and browse on lower branches. Partridgeberries grow partly hidden beneath the needles on the forest floor; the holly-like berries provide feed for animals and a little color for evergreen wreaths. Below the decaying pine needles, millions of mites make their homes, and mushroom spores and moth pupae seek protection from the frost.

Poet T. S. Eliot wrote, "April is the cruellest month"; he must have wintered in Florida. January in New England can be very cruel indeed. The month begins with only nine hours of daylight, and the average temperature is a blustery 29 degrees. Brown bats, bears, and jumping mice are snug in their weatherproof hibernacula. Baltimore orioles, ruby-throated hummingbirds, and other migrants have retreated to Mexico, Panama, and points south.

But the nippy weather is not without its attractions. About a dozen snowy owls are down from the Arctic, wintering over in the marshes around Logan Airport. These large white owls are attracted by the landscape—great treeless expanses with short grass and rolling hills that look like their home turf on the tundra—and the abundance of prey nearby: chubby rats, and flocks of nutritious mergansers, buffleheads, and black ducks that float in rafts on the marshes. Pigeons are easy picking, too. Like Davy Crockett, the snowies sleep with one eye open. They do most of their hunting during the night. You're most likely to see them early in the morning or late in the afternoon, sweeping silently over the marshes on their five-foot wings, taking most of their victims in flight.

And thus another new year begins in the month of the Wolf Moon, when the days are short and cold, the woods are empty, and ponds are rimmed with ice. Shouldn't we be celebrating the New Year in the spring, when the days are long, the flowers are in bloom, and the birds are twittering in leaf-filled trees?

Well, that was once the case. The ancient Celts and early Colonists celebrated the New Year in March, on or about the first day of spring. That all changed in 1751, when we accepted the Gregorian calendar.

The Gregorian calendar, adopted at the behest of Pope Gregory XIII, replaced the Julian calendar decreed by Julius Caesar. The Julian Calendar was an inaccurate instrument: it was 11 minutes and 14 seconds longer than the solar year. This time added up. By the sixteenth century, the winter and summer solstices were off by weeks, and more important, Easter was bearing down on summer. The Vatican stepped in and adopted the Gregorian Calendar, which more accurately reflects the solar year. In keeping with Christian values, and the celebration of Christmas and Advent, it was decreed that the New Year begin on January 1.

CALENDAR

Jan. 1

The delicate, four-legged water strider that dappled the surface of Furnace Brook in Quincy, Massachusetts, is wintering over in the muck at the bottom of the water.

Jan. 2

A saw-whet owl perches on an oak tree in a woodlot in Meriden, Connecticut. This small, six-inch-tall owl is brown and white with yellow eyes. Like most owls, saw-whets are nocturnal and rarely seen, but they're out there, often living surprisingly close to humans. If you approach one of these predators quietly when it is roosting in the daytime, it may snap its beak in a mild expression of annoyance at the disturbance. Native Americans associated owls with impending death and travel of the soul to the hereafter.

Jan. 3

Slithery, luxuriantly coated river otters are still active in an ice-choked stream in the shadow of Mount Monadnock in New Hampshire. These social animals often travel in pairs and appear to enjoy sliding down mudbanks and snowy slopes. Cross-country skiers may spot their slides along river-banks.

Jan. 4

Attitude is everything. The Earth reaches its closest point to the Sun, about 91 million miles. But, because the Earth tilts on its axis, those of us in the northern hemisphere experience our coldest weather at this time of year.

Jan. 5

Polaris, the North Star— not the brightest, but the best-known star in the night sky—is at its post one degree from the true celestial north pole. For

River otters

centuries, this star in Ursa Minor ("Little Bear") has shown travelers the way home.

Jan. 6

Twelfth Night, when the ancients thought animals could talk.

Jan. 7

Beneath the backyard, a chipmunk awakes for an acorn snack. This small ground squirrel's body fat won't carry it through winter, so it often awakens to munch on the nuts and berries it collected earlier in the year. Chipmunk burrows are up to 12 feet in length; they may include a storage chamber, sleeping room, refuse center, and latrines, as well as several well-concealed exits.

Jan. 8

A cardinal crashes into a window of a house built on a marsh in Newport, Rhode Island. Dazed, the bird flies up and crashes into the window again. Each year, millions of birds crash into windows of houses, shopping malls, office buildings, and phone booths. It's their number-one killer.

Jan. 9

A male ring-necked pheasant browses along the tracks of the B&M Railroad in Saco, Maine. With its red eye patch, brilliant iridescent green head, and chestnut brown plumage, it looks like it doesn't belong there, and it doesn't. Pheasants were imported from China for the sport of Victorian hunters. They're very tolerant of man and some now make their home in the city.

Jan. 10

A ratlike opossum drags its long, prehensile tail through the backyard. Possums are active all winter, mainly at night. These recent arrivals from the South often lose appendages to frostbite during the long New England winter.

Opossum

talons penetrate the crow's body and kill the bird even as it falls, squawking and confused. In daylight, crows may mob a dozing owl and create a fearful racket.

Jan. 15

An immature bald eagle, whose head has yet to turn white, follows the Connecticut River south into Massachusetts with strong, deliberate wing beats. The crimson setting sun reflects off the ice on the riverbanks as the bird scans the surface of the open water for fish. Dozens of these large raptors now winter over in Massachusetts, most of them on the Quabbin Reservoir.

Jan. 11

A shiny-leaved holly tree provides a rare patch of green on the edge of a clearing in Plymouth. Native Americans often planted holly trees near their homes, as a symbol of courage and eternal life.

Jan. 12

On this date in 1981, the temperature reached a bone-numbing 35 degrees below zero in a frigid hollow in Chester, Massachusetts.

Jan. 13

A pine marten stalks a cedar bog in Bolton, Vermont. About two feet long, nearly half of it tail, with gorgeous chestnut-colored fur, this pint-sized predator subsists mainly on squirrels, rabbits, and mice.

Jan. 14

At night, a great horned owl may seize one of thousands of sleeping crows in a grove near Shopper's World in Framingham, Massachusetts. The owl's sharp

Jan. 16

With the trees bare of leaves, it's a good time to spot a squirrel's nest, or "drey." They're big spheres of leaves about the size of a basketball. In cold weather, the squirrels usually abandon them and den inside trees.

Jan. 17

Greater scaup gather in harbors and bays in great rafts rolling on the swells; thousands of bobbing birds with light gray bodies and dark heads, chests, and tails. These ducks dive under water to gather mussels and other sea life. They will remain on open waters near shore until well into spring.

Jan. 18

A common murre—a two-foot-long seabird with a black head and back and a white chest—rests on a bush-lined kettle pond in Brewster, Massachusetts, where it was blown from its wintering grounds by a storm. When gales blur the distinction between water and air, birds that rest on the water risk drowning. So seabirds ride out the storm in the air and run the risk of ending up well beyond the usual limits of their range. Some stranded birds reorient themselves; others do not.

Jan. 19

Chickadees are active all winter. When the tiny birds are in motion, their little hearts beat 1,000 times a minute. In cold weather, they often sleep in cavities they chip out of punky, dead trees with just enough room for the bird to step in and fluff up its feathers for insulation.

Jan. 20

St. Agnes' Eve, when virgins are said to get visions of their future husbands, and the weather often turns from the bitter chill of early winter to milder weather—a brief but welcome January thaw.

Jan. 21

Most insects spend the winter as eggs, many of them laid in the crinkled bark of trees. Downy woodpeckers and nuthatches pluck the eggs from crannies in the wrinkled bark.

Bald eagle

Jan. 22

A maple tree creaks in the wind. The plant has been freeze-dried for the winter. At first frost, the water in the tree's cells migrates to intercellular spaces. The cells shrink and the solids left behind have a higher tolerance for freezing. But minus 40 degrees is the limit.

Jan. 23

The third week in January is quiet in avian circles in New England. There are no migrations to speak of; there are no huge shifts in population—just birds moving around to feed. The week of the great winter torpor.

Jan. 24

Starlings in Nashua perch on the chimneys of barracks built for the mill-workers, taking advantage of the warmth.

Jan. 25

Great horned owls—the first local birds to mate—are hooting love songs in the woods just beyond the city lights of Portland, Maine. Two feet tall with a five-foot wingspan, the yellow-eyed predator ranges in color from almost white to a more typical dark brown or gray. The owls will be raising young in the nest in late February, but it won't be until next August that the young become competent ratters themselves.

Great horned owl

Jan. 26

Take a good look at the moon and see if there's a corona, or ring, around it. The corona is caused by the refraction of light through ice crystals. If the circle expands during the night, you're probably in for snow.

Jan. 27

Downy woodpeckers are active at this time of year. They are black and white; the males have a red patch on the nape of the neck. Watch for them at dawn and dusk as they search for insect larvae under the bark of dead branches.

Jan. 28

Out where the decaying cornstalks poke through the melting snow, one fox is joined by another. Normally solitary animals, they make an exception at this time of year; it's mating season.

Jan. 29

During warm spells, skunks set off on nocturnal ramblings in search of food. They often commandeer one another's dens and sleep over there before returning home the following night.

Jan. 30

Great rafts of sea ducks bob on the frigid seas, apparently indifferent to the cold, feeding on mussel beds off Vinalhaven, Maine. A special network of blood vessels in ducks and gulls allows the arterial blood to warm the venous blood on its way back to the heart. A gull standing in icy water may lose 1.5 percent of its body heat through its feet. On land, gulls and other birds often draw one leg up closer to their bodies, conserving heat.

Jan. 31

The double-crested cormorants of summer have flown south. They are replaced by their larger, look-alike cousins, the great cormorants of the north. The size of a goose, a great cormorant is black with a white throat and a yellow chin pouch. Cormorants must unfurl their wings to dry, even in the cold winds of Boston Harbor. In Japan, they are sometimes kept on tethers by commercial fishermen, who remove the birds' catch after each dive, before they can swallow the fish.

Sea ducks

FEBRUARY. MIDWINTER. ICE. SNOW. LIFELESS TREES IN a forest as barren as a desert. This is the month of the Hunger Moon, when the snow wears out its welcome.

Snow forms when a supercooled droplet of water forms an ice crystal around a minute piece of dust, volcanic ash, or other particle floating in the air. Although each snow crystal is unique, the crystals are almost always hexagonal in shape. A few fall to the ground in their original shape, particularly in very cold regions like the Arctic.

More often, the ice grows into a snow crystal increasing in size as water vapor freezes around it. The snow crystal's shape is determined by the air temperature and the amount of water vapor in the air. As they descend, they bump into one another and merge, forming the aggregations we know as snowflakes. Sometimes the crystals merge with a frozen drop of water to become snow pellets.

Freshly fallen snow is a loose collection of snow crystals and air. It's a lot like a loaf of Wonder Bread: mostly air. If you were to squeeze the air out of a loaf of Wonder Bread, you could reduce it to a 2-inch cube. The same is true for snow. About 6 inches of heavy, wet snow or about 30 inches of dry, fluffy snow will contain as much water as 1 inch of rain.

Some say the Inuit people, sometimes called Eskimos, have a hundred words for snow. The English language also has about a hundred: graupel, needles, sheaths, columns, cups, plates, dendritic crystals, and hollow bullets are just a few of the dozens of names specialists use for snow, depending on its properties; and that doesn't include the unprintable names that commuters use for the road-clogging white stuff.

While white-knuckled commuters and grim-faced sidewalk shovelers may have had their fill of the white stuff, some critters don't resent it; they revel in it. The residents of the forest floor depend on a thick layer of snow for warmth and protection.

In winter, heat radiates from the ground to the cooler air above. A blanket of snow allows the ground to hold in that heat, so it rarely gets colder than 32 degrees Fahrenheit at ground level—and it's a lot brighter under there than you might think. The residents of this subnivean zone thrive in the leaf litter and logs under the snow, where the temperature is relatively balmy.

Foxes, wolverines, ruffed grouse, and other animals sometimes take advantage of the situation to burrow into a snowbank for a warm night's sleep.

The snow doesn't cover the ground completely. In empty spaces near rocks and logs, animals create systems of tunnels where red squirrels, shrews, meadow voles, and other rodents find warmth and protection from hawks, owls, weasels, cats, and other predators.

Red squirrels, those chattery residents of the coniferous forest, construct an extensive system of tunnels under the snow, where they feed on caches of pinecones stored during the autumn.

The mouselike meadow vole creates a web of tunnels from its den to caches of food. As many as six of these normally solitary animals will den together to share body heat, making them easy prey for weasels that stalk them by sound. After feeding on voles, a weasel may use their fur to insulate its burrow.

Shrews also reside in the twilight zone, but they're good diggers and seek insects in tunnels made by other animals. In snowless winters, these animals find themselves out in the cold and exposed to the unwanted attentions of hawks, owls, cats, and other predators. Turtles freeze to death in their nests in the sand near ponds and riverbanks, and rabbits are more likely to fall victim to dogs and coyotes because their white winter coats no longer provide camouflage against the bare ground.

A lack of snow is also bad news for field mice; they have to find safer quarters in cellars and attics. You may hear them skittering around at dawn.

It may be spring that makes a young man's fancy turn to thoughts of love, but it's the gray days of February that set an animal's heart aflutter.

The gray squirrels scrambling from tree to tree and digging in the yard in search of the acorns they buried last fall take time out now to fulfill the biological imperative. This early breeding season, combined with their short gestation period, ensures that their young will be born when the weather first turns warm, maximizing their chances of survival. The foxes skirting civilization in the suburbs trot through forest and field in search of a mate. During breeding season, their lust counteracts their normal caution around humans. Great horned owls hoot their mating calls in the deep woods. Bobcats also are looking for love; you might hear them yowling in the middle of the night.

On warm days, skunks venture out of their winter dens under porches and woodpiles to search for mates. In the salt water shallows, the male mallards and wood ducks that have hunkered down for winter chase each other across the water as they jockey for the attention of females.

Gray seals don't wait for warmer weather to breed. Their pups were born on secluded rocks off the coast and have already been weaned.

The skies are clear and cold. It's a good time to take a look at our home galaxy—the Milky Way. Best viewing is at the time of the new moon, when the sky is relatively dark.

The Milky Way is a spiral galaxy, about 100,000 light years across. To someone far above it, it would resemble a huge pinwheel with a bulge at its center. From our viewpoint, about a quarter of the way from its center in the constellation Sagittarius, we can't see the spiral because we're looking at it edge-on, as if we were viewing a plate from its side. We see only a milky strip of light.

There are several billion stars in our galaxy. Much of the mass of the galaxy is located at its center, where the stars are about 100 times closer together. The closest star to us is Proxima Centauri, which is in the southern hemisphere constellation of Centaurus. It takes its light about four years to reach us. It takes 8.3 minutes for light to reach us from the sun.

Our entire solar system is orbiting the galaxy in the direction of the constellation Cygnus. It takes about 250 million years to complete that orbit. The last time we were spinning hereabouts, man had yet to make his appearance and dinosaurs still stalked the Earth.

While you're viewing the Milky Way, the Earth is spinning eastward at 770 miles per hour, it's circling the sun at about 66,000 miles per hour, and our solar system is circling the nucleus of the galaxy at 155 miles per second. And you thought you were standing still.

Winter is half over. That's of little interest to most of us, snuggled in front of the TV set in our centrally heated homes, but it was much more important to our ancestors, who spent a lot more time outdoors, were more dependent on agriculture, and had plenty of time on their hands as they waited out the cold weather.

To them, February 2, the midway point of winter, was an appropriate time to wonder about the weather ahead, and whether they'd be doing the spring planting early or late. They understood little of the workings of nature and attributed much to the doings of good or evil spirits. They looked to animals and other signs in nature for guidance.

Since badgers and bears are rarely seen outside their dens in winter, it was thought that they had some special instinctive insights about how much longer winter would last. If the weather was sunny when the animals first emerged, they returned to their burrows. If it was cloudy when they emerged, they remained outside and went about their business.

When our ancestors took note of this behavior, they didn't consider the fact that when animals emerged into bright sunlight after having their eyes closed for a couple of months, the blinding sunlight hurt their eyes and they returned to their burrows to adjust; nor did observers consider that if hibernating animals emerged on a cloudy day, they might den up again whenever cold weather returned.

Thus, they came to believe that if a badger saw its shadow on February 2, it meant six more weeks of winter; if it didn't, spring would arrive early.

It was balderdash, of course, but our ancestors believed it, and when their descendants crossed the Atlantic to New England, they brought the superstition with them. But groundhogs were easier to find in the New World than badgers, so they became the prognosticators.

Feb. 1

Canada geese dabble along the first fairway of the Vesper Country Club in Tyngsborough, Massachusetts. About 40,000 Canada geese don't bother to migrate to Chesapeake Bay; they winter over near open water in the Bay State. Each goose defecates between a half pound and three pounds a day, raising the blood pressure of slimy-soled duffers.

Feb. 2

Pagans observe Imbolc, when ewes begin lactating and winter turns the corner toward spring. Christians observe Candlemas, the blessing of candles. As any hearty New Englander will tell you, it's really Groundhog Day.

Canada goose

Feb. 3

A Norway rat skitters into a cellar of a rickety tenement in Worcester. These rats are native to east Asia and Japan, where they live along streams. They were first seen in Europe in 1553 and probably arrived there in ships. They were first reported in America about 1775.

Feb. 4

A frog snuggles under a log in Keene, New Hampshire. When the temperature plunges below freezing, the hibernating amphibian doesn't freeze because his body produces glycerol, an alcohol found in commercial antifreezes.

Feb. 5

On a warm night, a raccoon sniffs out a trash can in Pawtucket, Rhode Island. You're 30 times more likely to see one of the amazingly adaptive omnivores in the suburbs or the city than in the woods. Raccoons have been known to ride trash trucks from town to town, presumably by accident.

Feb. 6

The Great Blizzard of '78 dropped 26.3 inches of snow on top of a big snow two weeks before. Military helicopters roared over miles of cars trapped on Route 128. New England shut down.

Feb. 7

Monomoy Island, south of Cape Cod's elbow, hosts one of the largest gatherings of harbor seals in the United States. Up to 3,000 of the dog-faced fish-eaters loaf and feed, waiting for spring.

Feb. 8

Folklore tells us that February fog means frost in May.

Feb. 9

In 1913, the Great Meteor Procession. Several hundred meteors were sighted streaking across the sky from Bermuda to Saskatchewan, taking three minutes to complete the full arc.

Feb. 10

Flying with the jerky motions of a wind-up toy, a house sparrow with a black throat and white cheeks homes in on a backyard birdfeeder in Springfield, Massachusetts. The aggressive, ubiquitous bird is a descendant of eight pairs released in New York in 1850 by Nicholas Pike, director of the Brooklyn Institute of New York. Pike introduced the house sparrow as a biological control for measuring worms, a destructive tree pest. Since 1850, the bird's population has exploded into the millions, taking the nesting sites of the less aggressive bluebird.

Feb. 11

A great horned owl, or "tiger of the night," perched high in a pine tree in Baxter State Park in Maine issues its love call: *hoo, hoo—hoo, hoo, hoo.* A larger, deeper-voiced female may answer him. In favorable nesting areas, as many as four pairs will set up adjoining nesting territories, hooting most of the night to ruthlessly enforce the boundary lines of their territories. Crows screech and mob a solitary owl but have to be careful.

Feb. 12

Four-inch ice needles lift a patch of earth and mud at the edge of Touisset Marsh in Warren, Rhode Island. The crystals grow up out of the ground when the air temperature is below freezing but the Earth's surface is not. The needles can grow to six inches high and lift leaves, stones, and small plants.

Feb. 13

Oxygen-starved trout congregate at holes in the ice, where they're easily picked off by otters.

Feb. 14

It's Valentine's Day, when birds allegedly begin seeking their mates.

Ice needles

Feb. 17

Out on the driveway, oil seeps slowly from a loose gasket on the car. A single quart of oil can contaminate as many as 250,000 gallons of water, more than 30 people will drink in their lifetimes.

Feb. 18

Like a gang of thugs, a raft of immature mergansers stalks pogies off Carson Beach in South Boston. These diving ducks were once shot because sportsmen thought they destroyed too many game fish. It's now believed that the mergansers cull schools of fish, controlling overpopulation and allowing survivors to reach greater size.

Feb. 15

Bobcats scream and holler like alley cats in a swamp in the Berkshires. It's mating season for the elusive, nocturnal predators. After courtship and mating, the scrappy felines go their separate ways. Two to four kits will be born in about 60 days.

Feb. 16

In a spray of ice, a rabbit bolts from underfoot. Flight distance often depends on an animal's speed. Quick-footed animals such as rabbits and foxes let you get close. Slower animals such as beavers and woodchucks lumber for cover at 50 yards.

Feb. 19

The brown creeper—smaller than a sparrow with a stiff tail—glides across a tree trunk, winding down, round and round like a barber pole, picking at bugs only she can see.

CALENDAR

Feb. 20

A hungry ermine, or short-tailed weasel, preys on rabbits 10 times its weight. They seize the squealing bunny at the back of the skull and hang on. They eat up to a third of their weight daily. If surprised, a weasel will dash into the nearest hole for shelter, but being very curious, it will often pop out if you make a mouse-like squeaking noise.

Feb. 21

A flock of crows shares a squirrel killed by a car in the breakdown lane of Interstate 93. Like wolves, monkeys, and people, crows cooperate on their ceaseless hunt for food. Experts say there are many more crows than there were in Colonial times. Garbage and road-kill provide an endless supply of food.

Feb. 22

A cedar waxwing eats the freeze-dried fruit that still hangs from a crabapple tree in Truro on the Cape.

Ermine

Waxwings are pretty, crested birds that may show up anywhere, without rhyme or reason, even in the middle of snowstorms. The bird is named for the waxlike secondary wing feathers that look like crimson candles from an elfin Christmas tree. Waxwings are social animals. They sometimes line up on branches and pass berries from bird to bird until one gobbles it up.

Feb. 23

White-footed mice usually live in the woods, but they winter over in houses and barns. Their midnight skitterings gave rise to many claims of ghostly wanderings.

Feb. 24

In 1862, a blizzard on Georges Bank off Nantucket sank 13 fishing schooners. Some 122 fishermen died, leaving 73 widows and 138 orphans.

Feb. 25

Bay or salt cove ducks like the chubby, bulbous-headed bufflehead and puffy-headed goldeneye stay together in small flocks of 20 birds or more. Black-backed gulls are more likely to attack solitary birds who are sick and old and can't keep up.

Feb. 26

The first flush of color as the draping branches of a deep-rooted willow tree turn neon yellow.

Feb. 27

The first storm of the Great Snow of 1717—actually the first of four storms that lasted until March 5—began on this date and dropped 4 feet of snow in parts of New England. Ninety-five percent of the region's deer population perished.

Feb. 28

You can begin to see the light at the end of the winter tunnel. Today we have 11 hours, 11 minutes of daylight, 2 hours and 6 minutes more than on the Winter Solstice on December 21.

Buffleheads

MARCH IS THE MONTH WHEN WINTER LOOSENS ITS icy grip and nature's clockwork seems to speed up. Each day, the sun rises higher, lengthening its path across the sky, providing about three minutes more sunlight. The added sunlight forces the polar ice cap to retreat and reinvigorates New England's temperate climate.

The sweet smell of wood smoke hangs in the air as New Englanders fire up their maple sugaring operations, boiling sap into syrup, even sugar. Native Americans had few sweeteners, particularly ones that could keep for months without refrigeration. They boiled the sap down to sugar and called it "sinzibukwud."

According to Iroquois legend, sinzibukwud was discovered when an Indian chief threw his tomahawk into a maple tree one evening. Overnight, sap flowed from the tree's wound into a container below the tree. The following morning, the chief's mate used the liquid to boil meat for dinner, imparting a delicious maple sugar flavor to the venison. More likely though, a thirsty Native American sucked on a "sapsicle" of frozen maple ooze and discovered its sweetness. Maple sugar was a cash crop for the early settlers. The industry got a big boost in the days before and during the Civil War, when abolitionists bought maple sugar to avoid buying cane sugar from the West Indies that had been harvested by slaves.

In Alabama, robins sense the lengthening days and begin their long flight north. So do the sandpipers in Panama and the Canada geese on Chesapeake Bay.

Songbirds have begun to return, adding their joyful noise to the arrival of the sun each dawn. Red-winged blackbirds are noisily vying for nesting territory in local swamps. Hawks that wintered down south have begun to move north. You can see them resting in leafless trees along the Connecticut River and Route 93.

Most birds migrate at night, under the Sap Moon. That's why we don't see them, though you might hear the honk of the geese at sunrise as they look for a wet spot to rest in during the day. Some scientists think the birds migrate at night so they can use the stars for navigation.

The cardinals and blue jays that wintered over in New England have started staking out nesting territory in the suburbs. You can hear them at dawn. The first insects—snow fleas the size of black pepper grounds—bounce in the sunshine on the surface of snow.

The ocean gets a greenish tint from the bloom of millions of microscopic plankton on which much of sea life depends. Swans return to claim nesting territories on local ponds and ocean inlets.

As the ice melts, beavers emerge from their twig-roofed dens and make their first above-water circuits of their ponds, to determine how their wetland weathered the winter storms. The reinforcement of their dams for the spring floods begins almost immediately.

Groundhogs' heart rates ramp up from hibernation speed of four beats a minute to the normal 100 as they unplug their burrows along the Concord River and emerge hungry after losing half their weight during their long winter naps. Squirrels inscribe arcs on trees, playing gotcha before they mate. Raccoons become active again and rustle around trash cans in the middle of the night.

But, as any Berkshire hillbilly worth his spit will tell you, spring is just a fancy word for mud season.

Mud season meant a lot more to us in the days before asphalt and macadam, when travel was by horse and the animals sank up to their fetlocks in muck, but it's still a major event for the plants and animals with which we share the planet.

Mud releases the moisture in the once-frozen ground, allowing the sap to rise and nourish the buds in trees that will soon be layered with leaves. Acorns and maple seeds that languished in the leaf litter all winter bask in the mud, where they germinate and sprout seedlings.

Worms that wintered in the earth below the frost line rise to the surface to avoid drowning in the water-logged mud just in time to provide quick nourishment for the birds returning from their winter migration. Frogs and turtles that have wintered under a comforting layer of muddy insulation breathe fresh air for the first time in months as they wander off to meet their fate. And the first flower of the season—the magnificent, malodorous skunk cabbage—blossoms in swamps and wetlands. Its smell, like rotting flesh, is the first whiff of spring for the flies that pollinate the plant.

While we humans await the first official day of spring, it's open water that makes a duck's heart turn to fancy. Mallards wintering over on Chatham Harbor pair off and head inland to set up housekeeping on Houghton's Pond. Canada geese and red-breasted mergansers follow the

Merrimack River north to quieter waters, as does the solitary loon, who leaves its wintering spot on the water off Hull for New Hampshire's Squam Lake.

Skunks move along prehistoric trails that sometimes lead into the blinding glare of headlights. The smell of spring in New England is the stink of a dead skunk in the middle of the road.

March 1

Right whales are returning north from their wintering grounds down south. They migrate and feed relatively close to land. You might see one off Cape Cod if you're very lucky. Their slow speed, and the fact that they float when dead, made these whales—now endangered—the "right" quarry for early whalers, who manned lookout stations along the coast.

March 2

Black ducks congregate in rafts of thousands in the waters off the Rachel Carson Wildlife Refuge on Cape Elizabeth, Maine. These dusky dabblers were once familiar sights all along the New England coast. Their numbers are in decline as they mate with mallards, producing hybrids.

March 3

In the highlands above Medford, Massachusetts, a broad-winged hawk just up from South America perches on the top of a dead pine tree, where it can survey the traffic on Interstate 93 and the steel-and-glass Boston skyline beyond. The crow-sized raptors migrate

Baby squirrels

north in flocks of several hundred. They feed mainly on snakes, mice, and frogs.

March 4

Baby squirrels are born, naked as baby mice, in the hollows of trees. You rarely see them, because they don't leave the nest until they're nearly full grown.

March 5

Alewives begin to pile up off the Cape, waiting for the seasonal rise in water temperature in brooks and streams. When the water gets warm enough, they will swim up the creeks to lay and fertilize their eggs.

March 6

Mottled brown mallard hens swim in a defensive circle as a green-headed drake begins his mating display. The lovestruck drake shakes his tail, rocks his body up and down, and swims a few strokes with his head low to the water. He tosses water with his beak, whistles, grunts, and checks to see if the females are paying attention. They aren't. He moves on to the next pod of females.

March 7

Eagles begin to return to their nests on Lake Umbagog. The inscrutable raptors return to the same site each year, adding big sticks to their nests until they sometimes become so large that the tree breaks.

March 8

Time for the lovely mating ritual of the Norway rat. Unimpressed by a male's attention, a female retreats to her nest. The suitor waits patiently outside, occasionally sticking his nose inside to remind her that he's still there. But rat etiquette forbids him to enter. He regains her attention by performing a courtship dance accompanied by squeaks and whistles.

March 9

A shrew takes its six babies out for a walk in Woonsocket, Rhode Island. At the first sign of danger, the first baby grasps fur near the root of its mother's tail firmly in its mouth. Each of the other five shrewlings grabs the tail of the sibling in front of it, creating a conga line that marches in perfect step. Some naturalists believe shrews resort to this behavior to imitate a snake and thus ward off predators.

March 10

A fox gives birth to five kits in the cellar of an abandoned storefront in Holyoke, Massachusetts. The little ones will be weaned in nine weeks. They'll remain near their mother until late summer or early fall, when they'll disperse to set up their own territories.

March 11

We're not out of the woods yet. The Great Blizzard of 1888 dropped three feet of snow in Keene, New Hampshire, on this date. Boston got only rain.

March 12

We're not the only ones excited about spring. The brant geese that wintered over in Quincy Harbor break down into small groups and rocket along the coast, back and forth, back and forth, steeling flabby winter muscles for the long flight to their breeding grounds in the far north.

Atlantic white-sided dolphin

March 13

Northern Lights. We associate the dancing curtains of color in the night sky with the North Country, but the magenta display on March 13, 1989, was seen as far south as Central America. The magnetic disturbance knocked out electric power to 6 million people in Quebec.

March 14

The tiny dogwinkle, a common snail about 1 ½ inches long, patrols Crane Beach in Ipswich, Massachusetts. These tiny wolves of the intertidal zone devour mussels and barnacles by drilling into them with a raspy tongue.

March 15

The green shoots of fiddlehead ferns begin to poke out of the mud in swampy gullies along the Concord River. Fiddlehead ferns provided the early settlers with their first fresh greens of the season.

March 16

Torpedo-shaped Atlantic white-sided dolphins sport in the warming waters off Cape Ann. Black on top with dark gray flanks and a long, white oval blaze below the dorsal fin, these energetic animals are often associated with humpback whales. They are usually found in groups of 10 to 60 individuals; offshore, they can occasionally be seen in schools of 1,000.

March 17

St. Patrick's Day. The traditional day for the first robin to return to Boston.

March 18

This is the breeding season for hares. In England, a "March hare" is the paradigm of zaniness. Male hares, or bucks, work themselves into homicidal frenzies during breeding season and may fight rival males to the death. The bucks bound after does who race off at speeds up to 30 miles per hour. After mating, the buck may leap backward, high into the air, emitting a sharp hissing noise. By the time he lands, he's made a complete about-face.

March 19

The male woodcock, sometimes called the "timberdoodle," performs its remarkable mating ritual in a clearing in Bennington, Vermont. Woodcocks are goofy-looking, stocky birds with rounded wings and a long bill. In the early evening in a clearing in the woods, the male flies high into the air; then tumbles down in spiraling loops. If he performs well, a female will join him.

March 20

Gray seals by the hundreds are molting on the sand bars and rocks off Chatham on the Cape. It's a stressful time for them and they tend to be cross.

March 21

The first day of spring is on or about today. At the Spring Equinox, the sun rises due east and sets due west 12 hours later.

March 22

In the dunes of Wellfleet and north to Province-town, the earliest of the heath flowers are in dark reddish bloom on the Outer Cape. The dark-reddish plants are the broom crowberry, with its muted, petal-less flower.

Woodcock

Peregrine falcon and pigeon

March 23

Small flocks of narrow-winged killdeer fly in to claim nesting territory on open fields on the North Shore of Boston. You can spot a killdeer by its call—a repetitive, high-pitched *peep*. When the birds are nesting, the adults often feign a broken wing and scuttle across the grass, dragging the "injured" appendage, to lead interlopers away from the offspring.

March 24

A slate-gray peregrine falcon, the size of a crow, dives between glass and steel Boston office buildings at 150 miles per hour to catch and kill a pigeon on the wing over the oblivious clatter of commuters at South Station.

March 25

A female earwig, a slithering dark brown insect with pincers at the edge of its body, has spent the winter under leaf litter,

protecting her eggs. In spring, females appear with a dozen babies and help them find food—fruit, garbage, or mites—before setting them off on their way. They have never burrowed in anyone's ears.

March 26

As the water in local ponds begins to warm, olive-gray sunfish move into the warm shallow water. The males select and clear nest sites, using their fins to fan away the silt until the bottom is exposed. Sunfish usually make their nests in the open, where there aren't any overhanging rocks or trees. You can sometimes see their nests from shore.

March 27

A cottontail rabbit bears its young in a round, grass-lined nest. It's the first of three or four litters a year. Prolific reproduction is a survival strategy for these defenseless animals, which are preyed upon by nearly every creature with teeth and talons.

March 28

Chipmunks emerge from their winter burrows. During their three-year lifespan, these gregarious homebodies rarely venture more than 100 yards from their dens.

March 29

Pussy willows blossom. The shrub's flowers, or catkins, are male and female and grow on separate plants. The willow's bark contains salicin, which Native Americans used as a painkiller.

March 30

Stork-legged great blue herons lumber over the Merrimack River on heavy wings as they return to their rookery in Tyngsborough, Massachusetts.

March 31

Hepatica appear early in the forest in Lenox, Massachusetts. The shape of these delicate white or pale pink, three-lobed flowers looks like a liver to some. The plant was once used to treat liver ailments.

Great blue heron

APRIL IS THE MONTH OF THE SPRING RUNOFF, WHEN
the water from rain and melting snow enlivens
local rivers and streams.

Water was power to early New Englanders: the
power to move inland before roads were built, the
power to float logs down the Androscoggin River to
market, the power to run mills. In Manchester and
Lowell, during the spring floods, that power ran
unchecked, threatening jobs and homes when the
Merrimack River surged over its banks. We can only
imagine the settlers' fears, because in most places the
annual floods have been checked by flood control
dams, while other means of generating electricity and
modern forms of transportation have relegated the
rivers to commercial irrelevance.

In the far north, New Englanders took advantage of the high water to bring logs to market. In northern New Hampshire, woodsmen slipped logs that had been felled over the winter and hauled by horses across the snow into the raging water. With strong poles and hard bodies, the loggers muscled the logs downriver to the pulp mill at the falls in Berlin, New Hampshire. At the peak of the runoff, 50,000 cords of wood floated on the river. Tourists braved mud season just to see them. The development of the modern tree-felling machinery and the 18-wheel pulp trucks put an end to the river runs. The last was held about 1964.

Some of this spring runoff splashes over each year to create temporary vernal pools that will eventually evaporate in the spring sunshine. The algae that grows in these watery ephemera feeds fairy shrimp, amphipods, and cyclops crustaceans—big-eyed creatures barely two millimeters long that nourish the salamanders through their damp life cycles.

One rainy evening, when the air is warm under the Grass Moon, spotted salamanders emerge from the leaf litter and lumber across the forest floor to mate and lay eggs in the vernal pools, where they can cavort free from fish and other predators. Every year, the bulbous-eyed, bow-legged critters brave cars, trucks, and other human impediments and drag their tails to their mating grounds. They've been doing it for millions of years.

Salamanders may live 20 to 30 years, but they don't breed until the age of five. They rarely travel more than 1,500 feet in their lifetimes, so they are particularly dependent on their wetland habitats.

Some scientists believed amphibians were the first animals to venture out of water onto land. But their days may be numbered. In recent years, their populations have dwindled; the result, some say, of habitat loss, of water fouled by salt and petroleum runoff, and of the depletion of the ozone layer, which protects their shell-less eggs from ultraviolet radiation.

Mosquitoes and other insects also use the temporary pools to breed, safe from fish and other predators.

Salamanders and mosquitoes go about their business silently. Not so the spring peepers—tiny tree frogs barely the size of your thumb—who mingle seed and sperm packages to the accompaniment of high-pitched wails. The din becomes deafening as these suction-footed frogs raise a ruckus way out of line with their one-inch stature. Only the males produce the high-pitched wail that can carry as far as a mile. The chorus of spring peepers is one of the loudest sounds in nature and should be familiar to anyone who drives by a swamp at night. To many, the sound of spring is the eerie song of these tiny amphibians.

The *rat-a-tat* call of a chickadee breaks the pre-dawn silence. Its solitary song is joined by the musical twitter of a warbler, the caroling of a robin, and the scream of a jay. A stand of pine trees in St. Johnsbury, Vermont, begins to sound like a jungle. It's April, and the hills are alive with the sound of music as songbirds compete for attention. Ninety-five percent of the racket is made by males vying for nesting territory and signaling their availability for mating. A short song followed by silence and then a repeat generally means the bird is vying for a suitable nesting site. It's listening for a reply during the silence. A longer call—often more exuberant but without break—generally means the bird is trying to attract the attention of a mate. Scientists believe the chorus occurs just before dawn because it's too dark to forage for food and it's a suitable time to think about setting up housekeeping.

Birds go through hormonal changes, much as humans do. Once the birds are nesting, they quiet down. At that point, singing might attract the unwanted attention of predators.

April showers bring May flowers, but the blossoms that provide a brief splash of color on the forest floor this month are just as beguiling, if less enduring. The colorful blossoms of the spring ephemerals take full advantage of their brief moment in the sun to blossom and fade before the trees acquire leaves and block out the sun. The early settlers, who lived in a seemingly drab world before TV sets, color magazines, and synthetic dyes, celebrated these flowers in song and story and sometimes ascribed to them magical or medicinal qualities. The fact that they appeared before leaves shut out the sun and made the forest dark and foreboding only added to the luster of the short-lived flowers.

White-petaled bloodroot flourishes on the banks of streams. The root of the plant "bleeds" a reddish-brown juice that settlers used as a dye. Dutchman's-breeches—a delicate plant with lobed petals that look like tiny trousers hanging on a line to dry—were considered a love charm by the Menominee Indians.

More than 5 billion birds squawk and flutter as they migrate north to their summer nesting grounds. Though the majority of the continent's 800 species of birds show some migratory behavior, a large part of their journey takes place out of sight. Many birds take the trip under cover of darkness. Some larger birds, like hawks, swans, and turkey vultures, cruise at altitudes of 20,000 feet, taking advantage of cooler air and high-altitude winds.

You're most apt to see the birds when they flock up to rest and feed, perhaps at your backyard feeder or at natural resting sites like the Parker River National Wildlife Reserve on Plum Island. This protected area near Newburyport, Massachusetts, is an important stopover for migrating shorebirds, songbirds, raptors (birds of prey), and waterfowl. As many as 25,000 ducks and 6,000 geese will congregate there at peak migration.

Many birds won't survive the journey. They become victims of planes, trains, and automobiles or windowpanes. And once the birds arrive, they aren't home free. In areas where people live, the smaller birds have to survive the depredations of their most ferocious predator, the domestic cat, and loss of nesting sites due to invasive species and land development.

Silvery schools of herring swarm up streams in a quivering mass. Their appearance, seething up local rivers each spring, was cause for celebration. The alewife, our local herring, is 10 inches long. Schools of alewives thrash and swim upstream, seeking the ponds where their lives began three years earlier. The females are heavy with their tiny eggs, from 60,000 to 100,000 of them. The males seethe right along with the females to the ponds, where they discharge their milt nearby. Early European settlers wrote back to England that you could walk across streams on the backs of the fish in an alewife run. Nothing like it across The Pond.

In 1934, five weather observers huddled in a wind-wracked shack on the treeless summit of 6,288-foot Mount Washington. All day, they took turns climbing out on the roof to scrape ice off a wind-measuring device. At dusk, their persistence paid off; they measured a wind speed of 231 miles per hour—a record. "Will anyone believe me?" one excited observer wrote in a log. People did. This record gust of 231 miles per hour still stands as the strongest wind recorded on Earth.

Goldfinch

CALENDAR

April 1

All Fools' Day. "If it thunders on All Fools' Day, it brings good crops of corn and hay."

April 2

Easy pickings for the screaming, swooping gulls that congregate at the mouth of the Piscatauqua River in Portsmouth, New Hampshire, to feed on quicksilver schools of smelt as they begin their annual run upriver.

April 3

Box turtles with high-domed shells begin to come out of hibernation on Cape Cod and lumber off on bowed legs. The turtles have become scarce lately due to the loss of habitat, the pet trade, and close encounters with cars.

April 4

Over Salisbury Beach, a northbound sharp-shinned hawk snatches a sparrow right out of the air. It's the most common of the accipiters—hawks with short wings and long tails. Sharp-shinned hawks are intolerant of civilization and their numbers are dwindling.

April 5

In 1815, Mount Tambora volcano erupted in the Dutch East Indies, spewing 25 cubic miles of ash into the upper atmosphere. As the cloud of ash crossed oceans and continents, it blocked the sun and created wintry conditions all over the world, including in New England, where it snowed the following July. Yankees later called the year "1800 and froze to death."

April 6

A flicker a foot tall forages for insects on the lawn. It has a brown back with dark bars and spots, a black crescent on its chest, a white rump, and a red patch on the nape of its neck. The flicker is the only brown-backed woodpecker in the East and the only one that regularly feeds on the ground. During courtship, it drums on dead limbs and tin roofs to demand attention.

April 7

A record April snow—13.3 inches—fell on this date in 1982. It didn't stay long.

April 8

In Boston, this is usually the last day for a killing frost. In 1952, however, the last frost in the city was on March 17; in 1882, it was on May 3.

April 9

Feisty mockingbirds are setting up nesting territory. You might hear the noisy, robin-sized gray birds as they run through their repertoire of imitations, trilling the calls of chickadees, blue jays, and other birds in an attempt to make other prospective nesters think the area is overcrowded.

April 10

Humpback whales frolic off Race Point on Cape Cod as they return from their wintering grounds in the Caribbean. The 40-ton acrobats seem to enjoy slapping their great fluked tails in the water. When they breach, they sometimes stand straight in the air to get a look around before flopping back into the sea. The humpback whale got its name from its habit of arching its back out of the water in preparation for a dive.

April 11

Swallows return from their wintering grounds down south to dive-bomb insects over local rivers and roads. They will cover as many as 600 miles in a day as they feed relentlessly.

April 12

Bluebirds return form their wintering grounds in the southwest, where the

Mockingbird

Navajo prize their electric blue feathers. To many New Englanders, the bird's arrival is an indicator of true spring, but their number is dwindling as a result of development and competition from starlings and house sparrows.

April 13

Elegant, long-necked mute swans have returned to Whitman Pond in Weymouth, Massachusetts, where they will set up housekeeping for the summer. The swans will defend their nests aggressively, charging intruders and native nesters with necks down and wings flapping. They look exotic, and they are. Mute swans established themselves locally after being introduced from Europe.

Mute swan

April 14

A great horned owl two feet tall surveys its territory from a hemlock tree in Norwich, Vermont. This predator's eyesight is so good that if it were literate, it could read a newspaper 100 yards away. These owls tend to nest near tree trunks, where their mottled brown color helps them blend in.

April 15

Bears emerge from their dens in the Berkshires with their cubs. The 150-pound sow will keep her young with her until their second spring. The bear population—an estimated 2,000—is booming in Massachusetts. Some are moving into the suburbs and chowing down at backyard birdfeeders.

April 16

Anadromous alewives, or herring, school in the waters of Cape Cod, waiting for freshwater streams to warm up so they can make their annual run upstream to reproduce.

As many as 500,000 of the silvery, 10-inch fish will make the frenzied rush up the fish ladder at Stony Brook in Brewster, Massachusetts.

April 17

Migrating bitterns in the cattails. They have a slow, rhythmic bass call, *oong-ga-choonk, oong-ga-choonk*. Primordial and weird.

April 18

Bright yellow trout lilies, or "dogtooth violets," blossom in the woodlands. The three-petaled yellow flowers appear for two months and then disappear back into the roots, which revive next April.

April 19

Lawns turn green about now, once again requiring the ministrations of suburbanites, who have become slaves to the labor-intensive foreign invaders.

April 20

A sassy red squirrel chatters at an interloper in a stand of pines in Scituate, Massachusetts. These gregarious omnivores prefer pinecones, but they'll eat almost anything, including insects and young birds. The colonists called them "chickarees" in imitation of their staccato chatter.

April 21

A daffodil blossoms at the edge of the garden. It's pretty and appears fragile, but it's really one tough customer. Plant cells are remarkably strong and can withstand an internal pressure five times greater than that of an automobile tire.

April 22

In 1852, the spring runoff swelled the Merrimack River until it crested at a level 14 feet 1 inch above Pawtucket Falls in Lowell. "Francis' Folly"—a gate constructed two years earlier by James Bicheno Francis, chief engineer of locks and canals, and

derided as an unnecessary extravagance—saved the day. The gate wasn't used again during his lifetime, but it saved the city again in 1936, 40 years after his death.

April 23

A beaver fells a birch tree on a tributary of the Merrimack River. The animal might be a good dam builder, but it's not a great logger; if the tree falls too far from the beaver's pond, it will leave it where it lies and move on to the next victim.

Trout lily

April 24

Hay fever sufferers be warned. Oak, birch, and beech trees begin to release their pollen at about this time.

April 25

Oak-apple galls appear on the twigs of young oak trees. The galls—tiny, apple-like growths about two inches in diameter— are light green in spring and turn light brown and become papery in the fall. Inside the fruitlike growth are insect larvae that have hitched a free ride on the tree.

April 26

Bumblebees—large, fuzzy insects with a loud buzz and a seemingly aimless, bumbling flight—begin gathering pollen from flowering plants.

April 27

A horsefly speeds up to meet a mate. They've been clocked at 90 miles per hour in short bursts. They are one of the few insects with only two wings. Their method of flying is one of the wonders of nature.

April 28

A mourning dove sounds its somber *coo* from its perch on a telephone line in Newburyport, Massachusetts. The long-tailed, small-headed gray-brown bird is sometimes called the "turtle dove." Its presence signals the availability of water. Native Americans often followed the doves to a water source.

April 29

In a burrow on the back of the Concord River, a woodchuck gives birth to three babies. The youngsters enter the world wide-eyed and covered with fur, but they won't leave their burrow until July.

April 30

Walpurgis Night. The eve of May Day, night of the Witch's Carnival. The ancients burned bonfires all night to protect them from evil spirits they believed to be at the height of their powers.

Bumblebee

WHILE THE INTREPID SEEK OUT THE EXOTIC ON INTER-
NATIONAL expeditions and couch potatoes watch in
wonder on television, New Englanders need only step
into their own backyards to observe the bizarre and the
beautiful. Ants invade termite colonies while antlions,
or "doodlebugs," lie in wait. Peregrine falcons snatch
pigeons on the wing. Rattle-
snakes stalk mice. Minks stalk
frogs. And meteor showers
etch the night with fire.

These observations were
made with little more than a
sharp eye and a layman's under-
standing of the natural world.
Now get out there and take
your own backyard safari.
There's no telling what
wonders you might find.

sparrows, 72, 79–80; house, 18, 130
spartina grasses, 104
sphagnum moss, 74–75
spiders, 35, 97, 111; barn, 76; black widow, 54; brown, 18; fisher, 28; orb weaver, 65
Springfield (Mass.), 130
spring runoff, 146–48, 157
springtails, 97
spruce, red, 36
Squam Lake (N.H.), 69, 139
squirrels, 10, 27, 59, 70, 82, 110, 116, 137, 141; flying, 42; gray, 124; red, 97, 111, 123, 157
starfish, *Forbes asterias*, 32
starlings, 70, 78–79, 118
Stellwagen Bank (Cape Cod, Mass.), 14, 26
Stinson Lake (N.H.), 28
Stratford (Conn.), 39
strawberry, wild, 34
sunfish, 144–45; pumpkinseed, 25
swallows, 155; barn, 4, 22, 54
swans, 137; mute, 156
swifts, chimney, 15

teals, blue-winged, 72
termites, 27
terns, 11, 55
thrushes, wood, 2
thunderstorms, 34–35
toads, 97
trillium, purple, 14
trout, 5, 53, 97, 103, 130
Truro (Cape Cod, Mass.), 132
turkeys, wild, 86–87
turtles, 12, 84, 96, 97, 124, 138; box, 20–21, 154; Kemp's Ridley, 91; leatherback, 28–29, 38; snapping, 26, 41, 65, 79
Tyngsborough (Mass.), 128, 145

Vinalhaven (Maine), 43, 119
violets, 10–11

voles, meadow, 39–40, 123
vultures, turkey, 79

Wachusett Mountain, 60
walkingsticks, northern, 11
warblers, 149; blackpoll, 69; immature, 66; yellow, 55
Warren (R.I.), 62, 130
wasps, 28
water striders, 7, 97, 114
Waterville (Maine), 11
waxwing, cedar, 132
weasels, 79, 85, 88, 107, 123, 132
Wellfleet (Cape Cod, Mass.), 143
West Dennis (Cape Cod, Mass.), 36–37
West Stockbridge (Mass.), 38
Weymouth (Mass.), 100, 156
whales: humpback, 14, 26, 77, 92, 155; pilot, 92; right, 140
White Mountains (N.H.), 27
White River Junction (Vt.), 67
Winooski (Vt.), 89
wintergreen, 43
witch-hazels, 76
wolverines, 123
wolves, 9
woodchucks, 61, 65, 70, 82, 127, 137, 158
woodcocks, 143
woodpeckers: downy, 117, 118; flickers, 154–55; pileated, 29, 96–97
Woonsocket (R.I.), 141
Worcester (Mass.), 25, 88, 129
worms, 55, 138; blood, 41; earthworm, 18, 61, 82; fall webworm, 6, 53; green tomato hornworm, 52

yellowjackets, 52, 56, 82
yellowlegs, 72, 92
York (Maine), 80

ACKNOWLEDGMENTS

THIS BOOK COULD NOT HAVE BEEN WRITTEN WITHOUT THE HELP of many. My thanks to Jay Johnson, who found art in the commonplace, and managing editor Penny Stratton, whose patience and attention to detail went way beyond the call of duty.

I'm grateful to everyone who helped with the text. Kathy Bouchard pointed out that neatness counts and helped prepare the original manuscript, Barbara Stratton undertook a detailed, painstaking copyedit, and Lida Stinchfield proofread it all. Thanks to Bob Prescott, director of the Wellfleet Bay Wildlife Sanctuary, and Laura Liptak of the Blue Hills Trailside Museum, who read the manuscript for accuracy and saved me from myself. Thanks are also due to Laura McFadden, who created the elegant design, to production artist Anne Rolland, and to indexer Kevin Millham.

Finally, I'm indebted to the late Ray Murphy, the original author of the "Nature Watch" column, who trod the trail before me.